What the Bible Says About
Angels

What the Bible Says About Angels

A. C. Gaebelein

BAKER BOOK HOUSE
Grand Rapids, Michigan

Formerly published under
the title
The Angels of God
First printed in 1924 by
"Our Hope" Publication Office
Paperback edition issued 1975
by Baker Book House

ISBN: 0-8010-3697-6

Printed in the United States of America
by Dickinson Brothers, Inc.
Grand Rapids, Michigan.

TABLE OF CONTENTS

4

CHAPTER I

The Heavens and their glory.—Immeasurable Distances.—Sixty thousand billion miles.—Spiral Nebulae are agglomorations of suns.—Ancient nations and astronomy.—David's statement.—Is Man the only intelligent Creature in the Universe?—Are the stars inhabited?—Professor Lowell and Mars.—The answer from the Bible.

"THE heavens declare the glory of God; and the firmament showeth His handiwork" (Ps. xix:1). How marvellous these heavens are! It staggers the finite mind of man to listen to the wonder-story told by astronomy. It fills the heart with awe and reveals to man his own insignificance. Two hundred and forty thousand miles from our earth is the Moon, our satellite—so near, yet so mysterious. Light travels at 186,000 miles in a second, so that it only takes one and one-third seconds to cover the distance between Earth and Moon. Our next door neighbor in our solar system is the planet Mars. Mars is thirty-seven million miles from man's habitation. If supposed beings are dwelling there our Earth would appear to them as a brilliant star. Next we reach the planet Saturn at a distance of 750 million miles from us. Saturn's diameter is nine and one-half times larger than our own and this planet is surrounded by immense rings measuring nearly 200,000 miles across. 2,500 million miles from the Sun is the planet Neptune. There are other planets, still unknown, beyond Neptune, which belong to the outermost regions of our solar system. And beyond are the almost infinite heavens. There

25 billion miles from our Earth every star is a shining sun. "Whatever star we approach, we find in it a sun like a blinding furnace. These innumerable centers of light, heat, electricity and gravitational attraction only appear to us as small luminous points on account of the immense abysses which separate us from them. The nearest sun, our nearest star in space, burns at 276,000 times the distance which separates us from the Sun, i.e., 25 billion miles from the Earth. Travelling with the speed of an express train flung into space at 40 miles an hour towards the nearest star, without any stoppage or slowing down, we should not arrive at our destination until after an uninterrupted flight of 75 million years." But even this inconceivable space dwindles in view of the fact that in a distance of 60,000 billion miles there are other wonderful suns.

And beyond that? Another mighty universe. The spiral nebulae, which the powerful telescopes bring within human vision, are not, as once supposed, balls of gaseous matter, but agglomerations of suns, in such a distance and in such numbers that the finite mind of man is unable even to express it. "Then I understand that all the stars which have ever been observed in the sky, the millions of luminous points which constitute the Milky Way, the innumerable celestial bodies, suns of every magnitude and of every degree of brightness, solar systems, planets and satellites, which by millions and hundreds of millions succeed each other in the void around us, that whatever human tongues have designated by the name of universe, do not in the infinite represent more than an archipelago of celestial islands and not more than a city in a grand total of population, a town of greater or lesser importance. In this city of the limitless empire, in this town of a land without frontiers, our Sun and its system represents a single point, a single house among millions of other habitations. Is our solar system a palace or a hovel in this great city? Probably a hovel. And the earth? The Earth is a room in the solar mansion—a small dwelling, miserably small."*

The heavens declare the glory of God! And such a glory! From earliest times man has been occupied with the heavens and their unfathomable mysteries. Astronomy and astrology were the chief occupations of the wise men of Egypt, Assyria, Babylonia and other great empires of the past. The inspired pen of David, Judah's great king, tells us how he contemplated these wonderful heavens. "When I consider the heavens, the work of Thy fingers, the moon and the stars which Thou hast ordained—What is man that Thou art mindful of him? And the Son of man that Thou visitest Him?" (Ps. viii:3, 4).

He marvelled at the condescension of the mighty Creator, who called all these suns and stars into existence out of nothing, that He should be mindful of man, the creature of the dust. He felt what every intelligent human being must feel, that this earth is but a little grain of sand on the mighty shores of universes, and man, the tiny creature upon this little speck.

Here another question arises. Is man the only creature of God in this vast space, amidst these millions and millions of flaming worlds, who has a mind to appreciate and to contemplate these master works of God? Has God no other creatures of intelligence who

*Camille Flammarion.

praise Him for all His works and serve Him? Are these millions of stars without tenants? Is our world the only world upon which a race dwells with capacity to know God and His works? If man is God's only creature, gifted by Him with powers to search out His creation, to admire His works and to praise Him for them, how little is the praise and glory He gets from His creatures! The vast majority of our race, though walking erect, has only eyes for the things of the dust, and never thinks of Him who has created all. And, worse than that, countless thousands deny the existence of a personal God, speak of matter as being eternal, self-existent; and earth and the heavens as they are now the result of an imaginary evolutionary process, the when and how of which is still, and will always be, enshrouded in an impenetrable mystery. A very small part of our race worship and praise Him. Is it God-like to have fashioned universes with no other creatures in these heavenly depths to appreciate Him and His creation, than man dwelling on this little globe we call earth?

The question is an old one. The ancients thought of it. For centuries it has occupied some of the great minds of our race. Astronomers have been asked about other inhabited worlds and have given often an affirmative answer. Some years ago, during a stay in Arizona, the writer visited Flagstaff. We called on the widely-known astronomer, Professor Lowell. At that time, much was being said in the astronomical world about Mars and the possible intelligent beings living on that planet. Professor Lowell claimed that there is intelligent life on Mars. He had noticed through his magnificent telescope that certain lines on the surface of Mars were changing and he claimed to have discovered that somebody is at work in digging gigantic canals. He had taken many photographs showing the supposed activities of intelligent creatures. He showed us these photographs. When the time came for us to ask him a few questions to satisfy our curiosity, we found that he could not answer us. "Who, do you think, are the beings, living on Mars?" "I do not know." "What kind of a race are they, and have they bodies like ours?" "I do not know." "If there are real beings there, where did they come from?" "I do not know." So we came away, having admired the nice big glass on top of the mountain, and the fine photographs, but not a bit wiser than before. It has been almost universally conceded by the foremost astronomers that Mars has conditions which are suitable for life as we know it on our earth. Like our earth, Mars has dry land and oceans. The spectroscope has revealed that Mars has an atmosphere like our own; there is oxygen and nitrogen. Venus, also, it is claimed, has similar conditions. But who can tell of the other suns and their planets and their possible inhabitants?

From the guesses of science we turn to the revelation of God, the Bible. Does the Word of God answer our question about other beings in this immense space, which we call the heavens, who know God as Creator, who know His works and who serve Him? And if there are such beings in existence, who are they, where are they and what are they doing? The Bible is not silent on these questions. God's Holy Word gives us an answer. There is another class of beings above man. These beings are the Angels of God, the heavenly hosts, the tenants of the heavens, the innumerable company of the unseen servants of God.

CHAPTER II

Prominence of Angels in both Testaments.—Sadducees and Modernists.—Testimony of Christ as to the Angels.—Mythologies of other nations.—Angels a class of Beings above man.—The Sons of God shouting for joy.—The innumerable company of Angels.—The Archangel, the Seraphim and Cherubim.

FROM Genesis to Revelation the angels of God are prominently mentioned, one hundred and eight times in the Old Testament and one hundred and sixty-five times in the New Testament. They are seen throughout sacred history. Their activities in heaven and on earth in the past are recorded in both Testaments, also their future manifestations are prophetically revealed. There can, therefore, be no question as to the existence of these supernatural beings for the infallible Word of God speaks of them as such. The sect of the Sadducees among the Jews did not believe in angels (Acts xxiii:8). Modernism of today, the Twentieth Century Sadduceeism, also denies the existence of such a class of beings. Destructive criticism, which has given birth to Modernism, claims that the belief in angels must be traced to the period of the exile, when the Jews came in contact with Babylonian and Persian myths. Like so many other precious things in the Word of God, belief in angels is said to be of Babylonian origin. We do not follow these so-called "scholarly" inventions, which are aimed at the destruction of the Bible as our only authority. Over against all these denials we put but one witness, the Son of God, our Lord Jesus Christ. What did He have to say about angels? He confirmed the teachings as to angels in the Hebrew Scriptures. He spoke of them as real beings. In His kingdom parables He mentions them as the reapers at the close of the age. He spoke of them as associated with Him in His second coming. He rebuked Peter's action in defending Him in the garden by a reference to angels, "Thinkest thou that I cannot now pray to my Father, and he shall presently give me more than twelve legions of angels?" (Matt. xxvi:53). He described their very nature as well as their interest in what is going on in the earth (Luke xv:10) and that in the days of His kingdom they shall be seen ascending and descending upon the Son of Man (John i:51). Modernism gives an answer to these testimonies of our Lord, which dishonors Him in such a manner that we cannot be in doubt as to the source from whence these infidel theories emanate. They say that our infallible Lord, He who is the Truth, mingled with His instructions the erroneous notions of those to whom they were addressed. They claim, perhaps He knew, or perhaps He knew not, that angels never existed, but He accommodated Himself to the beliefs current among the Jews in His day. We add one more argument. As we shall show later, our blessed Lord, after His resurrection, was exalted in His glorified humanity to a place above the angels, receiving a more excellent name than they (Heb. i:4). Now, if angels are only imaginary beings and do not exist, then we might conclude that His exaltation and inheritance is also only imaginary and has no reality. Like everything else in Modernism, the denial of angels strikes at the Deity and glory of the Lord Jesus Christ.

The mythologies of nearly all the ancient nations speak of such beings. Babylonian mythology pictured them as gods who conveyed messages from gods to men. Roman and Greek mythology had its genii, semi-gods, fauns, nymphs and naiads, who visited the earth. Hesiod, next to Homer, the earliest Greek poet, said: "Millions of spiritual creatures walk the earth." Egypt and Eastern nations believed in such supernatural, unseen creatures. The belief is well-nigh universal. Mythologies are the faint and distorted echoes of a common primeval knowledge possessed by the race. If such beings of a higher rank than man did not exist we would not find them in the traditional beliefs of the nations of old.

The Bible teaches that angels are a class of created beings above man. Man is made a little lower than the angels (Ps. viii:5; Heb. ii:7). This disposes of another false conception. Some teach that believers who die, as well as children, become angels. Man can never be an angel, for angels are forever distinct from human beings. Man redeemed is not lifted in redemption to the dignity of an angel, but in Christ man is carried into a higher rank than angels can ever occupy. More of that later.

When were they created? The Bible gives no definite answer to this question. But there is at least one passage from which we can learn by inference that they were created in the beginning, when God created the heavens and the earth. When that beginning was, no scientist will ever discover by his research. Perhaps millions of years before man was put here the earth existed in another condition from what it is now. It must have been at the time of that original creation, when God created the class of beings whom we call angels. All was created by Him in the person of His Son, and for Him, including the invisible things, thrones, dominions, principalities and powers (Col. i:16).

In the beautiful words with which Jehovah answered Job out of the whirlwind, we find this hint as to the time when the angels came into being.

> Where wast thou when I laid earth's foundation?
> Tell me if thou knowest and hast understanding.
> Who set the measures thereof?   Dost thou know?
> Or who upon it stretched the measuring line?
> On what were the foundations made to rest?
> Or who laid then the cornerstone,
> When the morning-stars sang together,
> *And all the sons of God shouted for joy?*—Job xxxviii:4-7.

That Jehovah here refers to creation is perfectly clear. They were, therefore, in existence when God laid the foundation of the earth, when He first created. And as they beheld His wonders in creation, they shouted for joy. We must not overlook the name given to them. They are called the Sons of God. Six times we read of the Sons of God in the Old Testament and each time it means these supernatural beings (Gen. vi:2; Job. i:6, ii:1, xxxviii:7; Ps. xxix:1, lxxxix:6). But it must be noted that while angels are called Sons of God, they are never called the Sons of the *Lord*. It is in the Hebrew always *Bnai* Elohim* (Elohim is God's name as Creator) and never *Bnai Jehovah*. The *Bnai Jehovah* are sinners redeemed

---

*Bnai is the Hebrew for sons.

and brought into the filial relationship by redemption. The *Bnai Elohim* are unfallen beings, Sons of God by creation. The angels are the Sons of God in the first creation; sinners saved by grace are the Sons of God in the new creation.

Inasmuch as they are sexless, according to the testimony of our Lord (they marry not nor are they given in marriage—Matt. xxii:30), and therefore do not multiply as the human race does, they were all created at one time in the beginning. Scripture informs us that their number is very large. Daniel, in one of his night visions, saw them before the throne, "thousand thousands ministered unto Him and ten thousand times ten thousand stood before Him" (Dan. vii:10). John tells us of his vision, similar to Daniel's, "And I beheld, and I heard the voice of many angels round about the throne, and the living creatures and the elders, and the number of them was ten thousand times ten thousand and thousands of thousands" (Rev. v:11). Hebrews xi:22 speaks also of "an innumerable company of angels" (literally: myriads). Multitudes of heavenly hosts appeared at the birth of Christ, shouting once more for joy at the beginning of the new creation (Luke ii:13). How large their number is only He knows whose name is Jehovah–Zebaoth, the Lord of Hosts.

Scripture indicates that in the angelic world, this vast kingdom of light and glory, there are different grades and ranks. In Ephesians i:21 and Col. i:16 we read of principalities, thrones, dominions and powers, which exist in this unseen world. They are in the heavenlies.

We also know there is an Archangel. Christendom

speaks of archangels, and follows certain traditional, apocalyptic views of different archangels, but in Scripture only one archangel is seen. His name is Michael, which means, Who is like God? His name occurs three times. In Daniel xii:1, where his special work is mentioned in behalf of the remnant of Israel, here he is called the Great Prince. In Jude, verse 9, where we hear of him contending with the devil for the body of Moses, and in Rev. xii, where he appears as the victorious leader of the heavenly hosts warring against Satan and his angels. His voice will be heard when the Lord comes for His own (1 Thess. iv:17).

Then we find Gabriel in Scripture. Gabriel means, The Mighty One. Both Jews and Christians have also called him an archangel without any Scriptural foundation, for he is never called by that name. He is a very august person. He, himself, bears witness to his place in glory, for he said to Zechariah the ministering priest, "I am Gabriel, that stand in the presence of God" (Luke i:19). From the throne of God he was commissioned (besides announcing the birth of John the Baptist) to bring to earth two of the greatest messages which ever left the courts of heaven. When Daniel prayed his great prayer of humiliation, Gabriel was called upon to carry the answer to the praying prophet of God. So swiftly did he pierce the immeasurable space that it took him but a few minutes to reach Daniel and to interrupt his prayer (Dan. ix:21-23). But the greatest of all the messages any angel ever carried to earth was the message sent through Gabriel to the Virgin of Nazareth, announcing the coming incarnation of the Son of God (Luke i:26-38). The Cherubim and Seraphim are angelic beings of a very high rank and are always seen in connection with the throne of God. The Seraphim appear only in Isaiah's temple vision (Isaiah vi). Ezekiel and John in the Apocalypse (as living creatures, erroneously translated, "beasts") saw the Cherubim.

And, now, before we examine the Scriptures as to the nature of the angels, their bodily forms, their dwelling places, their ministries in the past, in the present, and their wonderful relation to coming events and their future glorious display in the age to come, we must call attention to the person so frequently mentioned in the Old Testament as The Angel of the Lord.

CHAPTER III

The Angel of the Lord.—Not a created Angel, but the Lord Himself.—The Metatron of Jewish tradition.— Hagar and the Samaritan woman.—Abraham in Mamre.—The Lord His guest.—Prayer for Sodom.— At Isaac's offering.—Jacob and the Angel.—The Angel, the Redeemer at Peniel.—In the burning bush.—Angel of the Presence.—Joshua sees the Captain of our Salvation.—Gideon and Manoah.— The destruction of the Assyrian Army.—The Angel of Jehovah in the Book of Revelation.

THE first time the word angel appears in Scripture is in the sixteenth chapter of the Book of Genesis. Hagar, the bondmaid, had been forced to leave the tent of Abraham; she fled from Sarai. "And the angel of the Lord found her by a fountain of water in the wilderness in the way to Shur" (Gen. xvi:7). This angel (Hebrew: Malach-Jehovah) is not a created being, but an uncreated angel. It is Jehovah, the Lord, who revealed Himself at different times in the garb of an angel and generally in the form of man. This Angel of the Lord is not a messenger sent from God, but a theophany, a manifestation of Deity. Jehovah, the "I Am," is the Son of God. We have, therefore, in the repeated appearances of the angel of the Lord very interesting pre-incarnation manifestations of the Son of God, our Lord. We shall see that in each case of the manifestation of this Angel of the Lord, the marks of Deity are present.

19

It is noteworthy and of great interest that the ancient Jews in their traditions regarded the Angel of the Lord, in every instance, not as an ordinary angel, but as the only mediator between God and the world, the author of all revelations, to whom they gave the name *Metatron*. They called him "the angel of the countenance" (see Is. lxiii:9), because he always sees and beholds God's countenance, and they speak of him as the highest revelation of the unseen God, a partaker of His nature and of His majesty. They speak of him as the Shechinah. A talmudical statement declares *"the Metatron*, the Angel of the Lord, is united with the most high God by oneness of nature", while another source speaks of him as "having dominion over all created things." The very ancient Midrash known as *Otiot de Rabbi Akiba* makes the following declaration about the Angel of the Lord, "The Metatron is the angel, the prince of the face, the prince of the law, the prince of wisdom, the prince of strength, the prince of glory, the prince of the temple, the prince of the kings, the prince of the rulers and of the high and exalted." These ancient Jewish sources identify, therefore, the Angel of the Lord, whom they call Metatron, with the Messiah and as one with God. This was also the view of later Jews. Malachi iii:1 sanctions such an interpretation, the angel of the covenant is Jehovah, and the Messiah is the Angel of the Lord.

We shall examine briefly a number of these manifestations of the Angel of the Lord. As stated in the beginning of the chapter, He appeared first to Hagar. His visit to her reveals the tenderness of Him, who in time came to seek and to save that which is lost. He found her by a fountain of water in the wilderness. Knowing all about her and her affliction, He asked, "Whence comest thou and whither wilt thou go?" He revealed Himself as the omniscient Lord, who knows the secrets of life, and made such promises which no created angel could have made. And Hagar called the name of the Lord, with whom she had been face to face in angelic form, "Thou God seest me." He had bared her secret and revealed the future. He is the same who many centuries later in incarnation met another woman at the fountain of water in Samaria and revealed her secrets and she too confessed that He is the all-seeing One. "He told me all that I ever did" (John iv:29).

Years later, Abraham sat in the heat of the day in the tent door. Suddenly he beheld three strangers standing nearby. He left his tent door and ran to meet them. Before one, perhaps the one in the middle, he prostrated himself and addressed him as Lord. There must have been some mark of dignity about this visitor that the man of faith recognized Him at once. His companions were two angels (Gen. xix:1). Abraham entertains the Lord and the Lord promises to Abraham a son. The two angels departed; the Lord tarried with Abraham, His friend. Then followed words spoken by Him. "Shall I hide from Abraham that thing which I do?" The same voice spoke in the upper room with disciples gathered about Himself, "Henceforth I call you not servants; for the servant knoweth not what his lord doeth; but I have called you friends, for all things that I have heard of my Father I have made known unto you" (John xv:15). Abraham's prayer of intercession for Sodom was addressed to the Lord as He stood in human form before him. Abraham knew Him in His glory as the judge, for he said to Him, "Shall not the Judge of all the earth do right?" (Gen. xix:25). Then the Lord left and went towards Sodom, where the two angels had already preceded Him. Remarkable is Gen. xix:24: "Then the Lord rained upon Sodom and upon Gomorrah brimstone and fire from the Lord out of heaven." The Jehovah on earth calls to Jehovah in heaven to execute the fiery judgment upon the wicked cities. It is He, who in the days of His flesh, said, "I and the Father are One," the same who in future days will judge the world in righteousness, for the Father judgeth no man, but hath committed all judgment unto the Son (John v. 22).

On the mount of sacrifice He appears again. Abraham is commanded to take his son, his only son, whom he loved and offer him for a burnt offering. And He who was present, who watched, who knew all things, who interfered when the knife was ready to slay, knew that He Himself, God's only Son, should be the victim when His hour had come. When Abraham said to Isaac, "My son, God will provide Himself a Lamb for a burnt offering," He knew He would be that Lamb. "And the angel of the Lord called unto him out of heaven, and said, Abraham, Abraham; and he said, Here am I. And He said, Lay not thine hand upon the lad, neither do thou anything to him, for now I know that thou fearest God, seeing that thou hast not withheld thy son, thine only son, from me" (Gen. xxii:11,12). This angel identifies Himself here with God. Abraham knew that it was the Lord, for he called the place "Jehovah-Jireh." And when the angel of the Lord called the second time He gave such promises to Abraham which no created angel could ever have made. The Son of God in the form of an Angel was present in this scene, the same who in His days on earth said, "Before Abraham was, I Am."

Jacob knew Him well for he had most remarkable manifestations of Him throughout his life of conflict, ending in final victory. When upon his dying bed, blessing Joseph's sons, the old patriarch said, "God, before whom my fathers Abraham and Isaac did walk, the God which fed me all my life long unto this day, *The Angel which redeemed me* from all evil, bless the lads" (Gen. xlviii:15, 16). He knew that the Angel of the Lord was none other than the Redeemer, the Holy One of Israel, as the prophet Isaiah so frequently called Him. He appeared unto him as the Angel in a dream, and then told him, "I am the God of Bethel" (Gen. xxxi:11, 13).

But the greatest manifestation of this heavenly being Jacob had at the ford of Jabbok. There he was alone. All at once a man appeared who began to wrestle with him. When day was breaking, the mysterious visitor asked Jacob, "What is thy name?" And he said, "Jacob." And He said, "Thy name shall be called no more Jacob, but Israel; for as a prince hast thou power with God and with men and hast prevailed" (Gen. xxxii:24-32). Who was He? Modern criticism suggests that Jacob had probably a nightmare brought on by his deadly fear of Esau. Jacob knew with whom he had been face to face, for he called the place Peniel, "I have seen God face to face." Hosea bears witness to it in his prophecy. "Yea, he had power over the angel, and prevailed. He wept and made supplication unto Him. He found him in Bethel and there He spake with him, even the Lord

God of hosts; the Lord is His memorial" (Hosea xii:4-5). He who was with Jacob, the Angel, the Redeemer, is the same who left the promise to His own, "Lo, I am with you alway, even unto the end of the age."

Moses beheld Him in the burning bush. The bush is on fire. The Shechinah-glory is there, but the bush is not consumed. Out of that flame came the voice of the Angel of the Lord. He was in the midst of the burning bush. Moses is commanded to take off his shoes, for he stands on holy ground, in a holy presence. And when that voice speaks and reveals who He is, Moses hid his face for he was afraid to look not upon an angel, but afraid to look upon God. The Angel of the Lord in the burning bush said: "I am the God of thy father, the God of Abraham, the God of Isaac and the God of Jacob * * * I Am that I Am." He told Moses, too, that He knows the sorrows of His people, that He sees their affliction and hears their cry, and that He will come down to deliver, to bring out and to bring in.

"In all their affliction he was afflicted, and the angel of his presence saved them; in his love and in his pity he redeemed them; and he bare them and carried them all the days of old" (Is. lxiii:9). The Angel in the burning bush is the same, who revealed Himself in creature-form as the I Am, the loving, sympathizing Christ, who is now at the right hand of God, and sees, and knows, and hears, who has all power to redeem and to sustain.

The same uncreated Angel, the gracious, loving Lord, was with Israel in the wilderness. He was their Guide and their Provider. He had brought them out of Egypt (Numbers xx:16). In the history of Balaam we meet Him likewise, and while the blind heathen prophet did not see Him, his ass saw the Being of glory.

He was with His people when they entered the land of promise. When camped in Gilgal, the place of self-judgment, where the reproach of Egypt was rolled away, Joshua took a walk and looked upon the mighty, almost impregnable walls of Jericho. All at once there stood in his presence a man with a drawn sword. Joshua was not afraid to approach and to ask him who he was. But when the man reveals himself as the captain over the Host of the Lord, the mighty leader of the heaven's unseen forces, Joshua fell on his face and worshipped, while the captain tells Joshua to do what forty years before He had spoken to Moses, "Loose thy shoes from off thy foot, for the place whereon thou standest is holy" (Joshua v: 13-15). It is the Angel, the Redeemer, the Protector of His people, who compasses them about. The great post-exilic prophet Zechariah saw Him in his first night vision in the same character as Joshua did. He appeared unto the young prophet in the figure of a man riding upon a red horse, who is followed by an army of horsemen, who are now ready to undertake for Jerusalem. The Captain of the host of the Lord is our Lord, the Captain of our salvation (Heb. ii:10), who will come again some day riding upon a white horse and followed by the armies of heaven (Rev. xix:11, etc.).

In the second chapter of Judges He leads to Bochim, the place of weeping. Not a created angel can speak like as the Angel of the Lord spake at that time; only the Lord Himself can use such expressions: "I made you go out of Egypt and I brought you unto the land that I sware unto your fathers, and I said I will never break my covenant with you. And ye shall make no league with the inhabitants of this land; ye shall throw down their altars, but ye have not obeyed my voice. Why have ye done this?" Later in the history of Judges He appeared to Gideon. There, too, He is called Jehovah (Judges vi:14). Gideon addressed Him as "*Adonai*," Lord, and begs permission to bring an offering. The Angel touches the offering with the end of his staff, and fire bursts forth from the rock and consumes it. Suddenly He vanished. Gideon is stricken with fear, when the Lord assures him, "Peace be unto thee! Fear not! Thou shalt not die." Yes, He is the same who made peace, "*Jehovah Shalom*," as Gideon called his altar, the Lord, our Peace.

Still more significant and instructive was His visit to Manoah and his wife announcing the coming birth of a son. Manoah asked Him His Name. The authorized version misses the meaning of the original text. The Angel answered not that His Name is secret, but that it is "*Pele*," which means "Wonderful." It is the same word which Isaiah uses, when predicting the Messiah, the Child to be born and the Son to be given, and that His Name would be "Wonderful." Manoah and his wife also brought Him a sacrifice (Judges xiii:19-22). Then the mysterious visitor did wondrously. The flame of the burnt offering went up toward heaven and suddenly the Angel entered the flame and ascended to heaven from where He had come. It is a remarkable foreshadowing of the mighty work He would do in His incarnation, that He Himself would be the sacrifice and after His finished work return to heaven.

It was this mighty Angel of Jehovah who destroyed the Assyrian army which threatened destruction to the theocracy (2 Kings xix:35). He foreshadowed thereby the future deliverance of Jerusalem, when at the close of the times of the Gentiles that city is again besieged, when all nations will be gathered against Jerusalem to battle. Then, the prophecy of Zechariah tells us, the Lord shall go forth and fight against those nations, and His feet shall stand in that day upon the Mount of Olives (Zech. xiv:1-4). Then will He destroy with the brightness of His Coming the wicked one. We also mention 1 Chron. xxi:16, "And David lifted up his eyes, and saw the Angel of the Lord stand between the earth and the heavens having a drawn sword in his hand stretched out over Jerusalem." In Psalm xxxiv:7 He is seen as the Guardian Angel, He who delivers. Rome has used this passage in her false doctrines that angels should be feared, worshipped and addressed in prayer. The Angel is Jehovah Himself.

When we read the last book of the Bible, the Book of Revelation, we find that the Lord Jesus Christ, whose full glory is revealed in this capstone of the Bible, appears again under the symbolical name of an Angel. It seems to be the object of the Holy Spirit to remind us that He is the Angel of the Covenant of the Old Testament, who acts again in covenant promises, remembering mercy in wrath, when the present age ends and the kingdom age is about to begin. In Revelation viii:1-5, He is seen in His ministry of intercession, offering the prayers of the Jewish Saints, who are suffering in the tribulation period, with which the times of the Gentiles close, and then He casts the judgment fire upon the earth. In Revelation x He is revealed as the mighty Angel, crowned with a rainbow, the covenant sign, His face, as it were the sun, and feet as pillars of fire. He stands upon the sea and the land. It is a perfect picture of our Lord, about to come to claim His crown right over sea and land.*

We have written all this to show that in our treatise on the Angels of God we must separate this Angel of the Lord, as He is the Lord Himself. We shall now investigate more fully what Scripture teaches concerning the angels and their ministries.

---

*For a fuller treatment of the Angel of the Lord in Revelation see the *Exposition of Revelation*, by the writer.

CHAPTER IV

Angels are Spirits.—Have they Bodies?—Entertaining Angels unawares.—Take on visible bodies for physical manifestation.—They also have permanent bodies.—Not bones and flesh.—Corinthians xv.—Celestial and spiritual bodies.—Christ's answer to the Sadducees.—Nature of bodies unrevealed.—Summary.—Where do they dwell?—The three heavens.

WHAT, then, is the nature of these wonderful creatures of God? The Word of God answers us that they are spirits. "Are they not all ministering spirits sent forth to minister for them who shall be heirs of salvation?" (Heb. i:14). This fact needs no further elucidation.

The question is often asked by thoughtful believers, have angels bodies? If they have bodies, what kind of bodies do they possess? The question as to the corporality of the angels of God demands, therefore, a closer attention. Not a few expositors of Scripture maintain that a spirit must be immaterial, that spirituality excludes corporality and, therefore, the angels as spirits are bodyless beings. We know from Scripture that they appeared in visible form, generally in likeness of a human body. It seems these unseen spirits taking on visibility could not always be distinguished from ordinary creatures. In an exhortation to hospitality we read in Hebrews xiii:1, "Be not forgetful to entertain strangers, for thereby some have entertained angels unawares." We learn from this that pious Hebrews in Old Testament times received strangers into their homes, entertained them, only to discover later that they were the messengers of God. We conclude, therefore, that they did not appear, as pictured in art, with wings and a halo about the head. They looked like as if they were common mortals. From other Scriptures we learn that their bodies sometimes possessed a marvellous glory. Their garments are described as shining, their faces like the lightning and their whole appearance in whiteness like the snow. How can this be reconciled with the assertion that they are only spirits? It is answered, that they possess the faculty of appearing in corporeal form at will; that they can pierce the universe at a speed even greater than the speed of light; that they can come and go unperceived by mortal sense, or appear visibly. There can be taken no exception to these statements. We also believe that these holy beings possess such a faculty of taking on bodily form and appear and disappear as they desire. But this is not the question with which we are now occupied. Have they as spirit-beings permanent bodies? It is not the question of their power to clothe themselves with such a garment that will make them visible to human eyes, but have they always bodies? This question we can answer from the Scriptures in the affirmative. The Bible teaches the corporality of the angels. They possess personality and, though spirits, they have their own distinctive bodies. That the bodies they possess are not like our own bodies may be learned from the words of the risen Lord. When suddenly He appeared in the midst of the disciples, they cried out for fear. "They were terrified and affrighted, and supposed that they had seen a spirit. And he said unto them, Why are ye troubled, and why do thoughts arise in your hearts? Behold my hands and my feet, that it is myself; *for a spirit has not bones and flesh as ye see me have*" (Luke xxiv:37-39). Our Lord, therefore, taught definitely that a spirit has not a body of bones and flesh.

In the great resurrection chapter, that is, the fifteenth chapter of the first epistle of Paul to the Corinthians, different kinds of bodies are mentioned. The Spirit of God speaks of terrestrial bodies and of celestial bodies. He tells us that there is a natural body and there is a spiritual body. Man received his terrestrial, his natural body, from mother earth. But angels never were clothed with such a body, for that is indicated in the statement of Scripture, that man is made a little lower than the angels. The angels, therefore, have spiritual bodies, that is, celestial bodies, corresponding to their exalted, glorious, spiritual nature. Apart from this general fact, we have more positive information from the lips of our Lord.

The Sadducees, those infidels of the past, who denied the existence of angels and also the resurrection, came and asked the Lord a question: "Master, Moses wrote unto us, if any man's brother die, having a wife, and he die without children, that his brother should take his wife, and raise up seed unto his brother. There were, therefore, seven brethren, and the first took a wife, and died without children. And the second took her to wife, and he died childless. And the third took her; and in like manner the seven also; and they

left no children, and died.   Last of all the woman died
also. Therefore in the resurrection whose wife of
them is she, for seven had her to wife?" (Luke xx:
27-36).   In all probability the story was of their own
invention to ensnare the Lord Jesus Christ.   The
answer He gave contains the information as to the
corporality of the angels: "And Jesus answering said
unto them, The children of this world marry, and are
given in marriage; but they which shall be accounted
worthy to obtain that world, and the resurrection from
among the dead (the first resurrection) neither marry,
nor are given in marriage, neither can they die any
more;   for they are equal unto angels, and are the
children of God, being the children of resurrection."
Here the Lord teaches that angels have real bodies.
The logical conclusion is that the angels have bodies,
but that these bodies are different from human bodies
in that the angels do not marry, or are given in marriage and that they do not die.   Here, also, is the
valuable hint of the resurrection bodies of the
redeemed;   the participators in the first resurrection
will have bodies, at least in these two respects, like
unto the angelic bodies.   Our resurrection bodies are
deathless bodies and the earthly conjugal relationship
will no longer exist.   The highest revelation concerning
the resurrection body of the redeemed is given after
the Lord Jesus Christ rose from among the dead.   The
Spirit of God tells us that our bodies shall be like unto
His glorious body.   As pointed out, our Lord speaks
of only two things in which our resurrection bodies
are equal to that of angels.   We learn from these
words of our Lord that angels have real bodies.

What kind of bodies are theirs?   This question is

unanswerable. Councils in early church-history held that their bodies were ethereal and firelike, while the scholastics and the Lateran Council decided that their bodies were material bodies. The synagogical literature of the Jews is rich in all kinds of suggestions as to the bodies of angels and strange traditional beliefs. Many rabbis declared that the body of an angel is fully described in Daniel x:6. But these are vain speculations. We have to own that we look into a glass darkly in connection with these unseen things. These things are for us in our present state unexplainable and incomprehensible. Beyond what is written we dare not go. The time will surely come when we shall not longer look into a glass darkly, when faith is changed into sight. Then the unseen things, including angels and their glorious bodies, will be fully known by us. What we know from Scripture are the following facts:

1. They are spirits called into existence by an immediate act of creation.

2. In coming in touch with man they displayed their faculty of assuming the human form at will, to appear suddenly and to disappear in the same manner. They also appeared in white raiment—white as snow, with a light of glory about them.

3. They have bodies. A creature without corporality is next to inconceivable. Corporality is the goal of all the ways of God. The Lord Jesus Christ shows that the resurrection bodies of His people will be equal to the bodies of the angels, which they possess now.

4. The nature of the angelic body is unknown for it is unrevealed.

In the next place we have to ascertain their *dwelling places*. As we have pointed out before, their number is so great that they cannot be reckoned. The unseen world of angels is a mighty kingdom in which are thrones, principalities, powers and dominions. Inasmuch as they are spirits clothed with bodies they must have fixed dwelling places. Where are the angels is therefore another interesting question which Scripture, at least in part, answers also. A child who has been taught something about the Bible will answer readily the question about the place where the angels are. The child will answer, "In heaven." But heaven is a term of vast meaning. In the Hebrew, heaven is in the plural, "the heavens." The Bible speaks of three heavens, the third heaven is the heaven of heavens, the dwelling place of God, where His throne has always been. The tabernacle possessed by His earthly people, Israel, was a pattern of the heavens. Moses upon the mountain had looked into the vast heavens and saw the three heavens. He had no telescope. But God Himself showed to him the mysteries of the heavens. Then God admonished him when he was about to make the tabernacle and said to His servant, "See, that thou make all things according to the pattern showed to thee in the mountain" (Heb. viii:5). The tabernacle had three compartments, the outer court, the Holy part and the Holiest. Once a year the high priest entered this earthly place of worship to pass through the outer court, into the Holy part, and, finally, carrying the sacrificial blood, he entered into the Holiest to sprinkle the blood in Jehovah's holy presence. But Aaron was only a type of Him who is greater than Aaron, the true High Priest.

Of Him, the true Priest, our Lord and Saviour Jesus Christ, it is written that He passed *through the heavens* (Heb. iv:14). "For Christ is not entered into the holy places made with hands, which are the figures of the true, but into heaven itself, now to appear in the presence of God for us" (Heb. ix:24). He passed through the heavens, the outer court, the heaven surrounding the earth; the holy part, the immense universes, with their immeasurable distances, and finally He entered the third heaven, that heaven astronomy knows exists, but which no telescope can ever reach.

In the heavenlies, according to the Epistle to the Ephesians, are the principalities and the powers, the innumerable company of angels. Their dwelling places are in these heavens. God who created them, who made them spirits and clothed them with bodies suited to their spirit nature, must have also assigned to them habitations. But what and where are these habitations? That these dwellings are in the heavens is not only taught in Ephesians. In the prayer our Lord taught His disciples is a petition which tells us of this: "Thy will be done on earth as it is done in heaven," that is, there are beings in heaven and they do His will. It is also significant and not without meaning that the phrase "the host of heavens" means both the stars and the angelic hosts; the "Lord of Hosts" has also the same double meaning, for He is the Lord of the stars and the Lord of the angels.

We shall learn much from the great catastrophe which took place long before man ever was created, when a great angel-prince rebelled and fell and with him a great number of other angels.

CHAPTER V

Lucifer, the Son of the Morning.—His glory and his fall.—He had a throne.—His original dwelling place, our earth.—The Scripture evidence (Gen. i:2).—Angels have their own habitations.—The Father's House.—What are the many mansions?—The Star Flower.—Christ in the midst.—In the Church.—In Glory.—In the Universe.—The great Worship.

IN the fourteenth chapter of Isaiah is given the description of the fall of this great angel-prince, whom some take to have been another archangel. He is addressed by the name of *Lucifer*, the son of the morning. Lucifer is taken from the Vulgate version which translated the Hebrew word *Helel* with the Latin Lucifer, light-bearer. The Hebrew word is best derived from the root *halal*, which has the meaning of brilliant, magnificent or splendid. This being then addressed as "Son of the Morning," perhaps the first creature, called into existence, was, as his name denotes, a magnificent, brilliant angel. This may also be learned from the prophecy of Ezekiel. In a message concerning the king of Tyrus, the Spirit of God suddenly addressed another person and spoke words which could never be true of a human being. Behind the king of Tyrus stood an unseen power, the master of darkness. To the once great Lucifer the following words must be applied: "Thou sealest up the sum, full of wisdom and perfect in beauty. Thou hast been in Eden the garden of God; every precious stone was thy covering, the sardius, topaz, and the diamond, the beryl, the onyx, and the jasper, the emerald and the carbuncle, and gold; the workmanship of thy tabrets and of thy pipes was prepared in thee in the day thou wast created. Thou art the anointed cherub that covereth; and I have set thee so, thou wast upon the holy mount of God, thou hast walked up and down in the midst of the stones of fire. Thou wast perfect in thy ways from the day that thou wast created, till iniquity was found in thee" (Ezek. xxviii:12-15). We notice he is called "the anointed cherub that covereth," which gives him another great distinction. This mighty and glorious person, Lucifer, the son of the morning, became a rebel. Isaiah gives us the story of his fall. "Thou hast said in thine heart, I will ascend into heaven, I will exalt my throne above the stars of God, I will also sit upon the mount of the congregation, in the sides of the north. I will ascend above the heights of the clouds; I will be like the most High" (Isaiah xiv:13, 14). He fell by pride. He exalted himself.

As we are not writing on Satan, the origin of evil, the fallen angels and the kingdom of darkness, we do not enter into this theme, but we point out certain outstanding facts in the passage quoted. Lucifer's ambition was to ascend into heaven, which must mean the third heaven, where the throne of God stands in its eternal majesty. He said again, "I will exalt my throne above the stars of God." He possessed a throne. The throne, which had been given to him by his Creator he wanted to transfer above the stars. Here again we find the evidence that his ambition was to be in the third heaven, for that is the heaven above the stars. *Now a throne demands a locality.* If a king has no kingdom, over which he rules, how can he have a throne? Lucifer had a throne and, therefore, he possessed originally a dwelling place, a fixed place in this universe assigned to him. This is strengthened by the next "I will," "I will ascend above the heights of the clouds." He dwelled then in a place which clouds covered.

The dwelling place of Lucifer, in his unfallen condition, was undoubtedly the globe on which man dwells now, the earth. Science has shown that the earth existed once in a different form from what it is now. There was here a gigantic animal creation and a corresponding gigantic vegetation. Man was not here in that distant past, perhaps millions of years ago. Science has never yet brought forth indisputable and conclusive evidence that man lived here ten thousand years ago, nor has science ever disproven the teaching of the Bible that man is the direct creation of God, in a class by himself, with a gulf between him and the animal kingdom which can never be bridged. Such a thing as the missing link never existed, and that is why it can never be found. All at once that original creation was wiped out by a great judgment of God and plunged into death, chaos and darkness. That state of the original earth is seen in the second verse of the Bible, "And the earth was without form and void; and darkness was upon the face of the deep." The word "was" has been more correctly rendered *"became."* God did not create the original earth in a chaotic condition (Isaiah xlv:18), for He is a God of order. The condition of the earth as seen in Gen. i:2 must, therefore, be the result of the fall of Lucifer, when he attempted to have the throne on this globe above the stars. He lost his domain, and when God created man, after having put the original earth into a condition to sustain a creature made a little lower than the angels, he appeared on the scene to regain his dwelling place. God had deposed him; he had become the prince of the power of the air, a wandering star, without a fixed habitation. The third chapter in Genesis tells the story of the fall of man. He injected his poison of self-will, self-exaltation into the head of the race. He had said, "I will be like the Most High," and he promised to the woman, "Ye shall be as gods." Through the fall of man he has been enabled to possess again this earth, and Scripture calls him now "the Prince of this world," and even more, "the God of this age."

But now to the point. Here is an argument for the belief that the angels of God have fixed dwelling places assigned to them by their Creator-Lord. Lucifer, as we have proven, had such a place and if he had a fixed domain it is perfectly reasonable that other angels have similar spheres—stars, if you please—in the heavens.

There is still another passage which proves this, even stronger than what we have written concerning Lucifer and his throne. In the epistle of Jude we find this significant statement: "And the angels which kept not their first estate, but left their own habitations, he hath reserved in everlasting chains under darkness unto the judgment of the great day" (Jude 6). To locate this event of which Jude speaks is not our purpose here. We believe, however, that this fall of angels is different from the prehistoric fall of Lucifer. We think it must be read and studied in the light of the opening verses of the sixth chapter of Genesis. The one thing we wish to consider is the fact, the outstanding fact, that these angels had "their own habitation." They had an estate given to them. This seems to us conclusive that angels have in the heavens habitations, places where they dwell, which they can leave as the unseen ministers of God.

Let us also remind ourselves of that beautiful word of our gracious Lord, which all His people love so well. "Let not your heart be troubled; ye believe in God, believe also in me. In my Father's house are many mansions; if it were not so, I would have told you. I go to prepare a place for you" (John xiv:2-3). It is true this lovely utterance of our Lord concerned first of all His soon to be orphaned disciples. He assured them that there is the Father's house, that He went there to prepare a place and then to come again and have them with Him in that place of glory. And ever since these words have been spoken they have comforted His sorrowing people and wiped their tears away. But who would deny that in the statement of our Lord there is a meaning beyond that it has for His own? The Father's house is a term which includes the whole universe. In that vast universe are many mansions, or as it should be translated, abodes— dwelling places. Man, as a fallen being, has no claim to any place in the heavenlies. The redemption work of the Son of God prepares the place for the redeemed, the blood-bought host. That place in the Father's house is the highest, the most glorious, as we shall see later. The Son of God, risen and glorified, brings

His many sons, purchased by Himself, into glory, the very glory of Himself. But what are the many abodes or dwelling places in this universe? The earth is but His footstool (Isaiah lxvi:1) and the clouds the dust of His feet (Nahum i:3). Is it unreasonable to suppose that these wonderful heavenly bodies we call stars are also dwelling places? Would it be reasonable to think that all these millions of worlds are mere ornaments, seen only by human eyes, and that no intelligent beings outside of the human race are in these universes to adore and praise the mighty Maker of it all? We cannot be dogmatic about it. We can only speak by inference. Angels are persons, they are spirits, they have a body corresponding to their spiritual nature. Furthermore, they have their own habitations, their own estates, where they dwell. These dwelling places are in the heavenlies; the stars are in the heavens. Where else can we locate the habitations of the innumerable company of angels, but among the stars? Many theologians of the past have expressed the same opinion. Yet, to find out if this is really so, we will have to wait for that happy, glorious day when we, with all the Saints of God, shall be caught up in clouds to meet the Lord in the air, when He Himself will introduce us to the mysteries of the heavens, which then will cease to be mysteries.

Last summer, we picked in a meadow a large flower, known as the wild carrot. It looked like a beautiful white star. The flower was composed of some thirty or forty smaller flowers, all forming a star, and each of these was also composed of a dozen or more small stars. It occurred to us that it might be named the "star flower." Then we noticed in the very center a single object, not a star, but something which looked like a tiny flower, of a purple color. All the star flowers were grouped about it. The purple object was in the middle. The longer we looked at it the more beautiful it appeared to us. Then we felt that even in nature are illustrations of Him by whom and for whom all things were created. We can see Him everywhere in creation, in the flowers of the meadow and in the stars of heaven. Like this purple center around which all the other star flowers are gathered, He is in the midst. Where two or three are gathered together unto His Name, there He is in the midst. It is His place and He delights in being with His own. His voice is heard in the worship of His blood-washed people, for it is written, "In the midst of the church will I sing praise unto thee" (Heb. ii:12).

He is in the midst in glory, the center of heaven, the heir of all things, the upholder of all things. All gathers around and about Him. Some day the impressive scene of the fifth chapter of Revelation will become history. Before the throne His people are gathered, when He only is found worthy to open the seven sealed book, He, the Lion of the tribe of Judah, the Root of David. John had a great vision, "I beheld, and, lo, in the midst of the throne, and of the four living creatures, and in the midst of the elders, stood a Lamb as it had been slain, having seven horns and seven eyes which are the seven Spirits of God sent forth into all the earth."

Here He is seen in the midst in glory. Then the worship and praise begins. It is a praise and worship before the throne in the heaven of heavens. The earth joins in and finally every creature which is in heaven, and on the earth, and such as are in the sea, praises and adores.

In this great worship scene we find the angels mentioned. "And I beheld, and I heard the voice of many angels round about the throne * * * and the number of them was ten thousand times ten thousand, and thousands of thousands, Saying with a loud voice, Worthy is the Lamb that was slain to receive power, and riches, and wisdom, and strength, and honour, and glory, and blessing" (Rev. v:11-12).

Perhaps in that day of consummation there will be heard the voice of praise and adoration from these dwelling places of the unfallen spirits, these mighty creatures and servants of God, grouped around the throne of majesty and glory, and upon the throne in purple, the color of royalty, He who was once mocked upon earth with the purple robe, but now enthroned as King of kings. But even now He is the object of praise and worship in the heavenlies. He alone is worthy and the angelic hosts know Him in their habitations in the heavenlies as the Lord of all.

CHAPTER VI

The Ministry of Angels in the third heaven.—The Seraphim and what they teach us.—Bishop Bull's remarks.—The Cherubim.—The sentinels of Eden. —Above the Mercy Seat.—Israel's camp.—In Ezekiel and Revelation.—Court Days in glory.— Job's revelation.—Satan the accuser.—Not yet cast out.—Another Court Day in heaven (1 Kings xxii:19-23).

The angels of God are seen in Scriptures active in the heavens and on earth. Glimpses of their presence in the third heaven before the throne of God and the worship and praise they render, we find in different parts of the Bible. In Daniel vii:10 we read of the myriads of angels who minister unto God. That ministry is the same which redeemed sinners are privileged to render—the ministry of praise. The Holy Spirit in the psalms calls upon angels to utter their praises. "Bless the Lord, ye his angels, that excel in strength, that do his commandments, hearkening unto the voice of his word" (Psalm ciii:20). "Hallelujah. Praise ye the Lord from the heavens; praise him in the heights. Praise ye him all his angels, praise ye him all his hosts" (Psalm cxlviii:1-2). Isaiah had a vision of what is going on in the presence of God. In the year King Uzziah died he saw the Lord. Above the throne stood the Seraphim. It is the only place in the Bible where these marvellous beings are mentioned. Isaiah gave us a description of them. "Each one had six wings; with twain he covered his face, and with twain he covered his feet, and with twain he did fly. And one cried unto another, and said, Holy, holy, holy, is the Lord of hosts, the whole earth is full of his glory." No wonder that the prophet in beholding such a scene cried out, "Woe is me! for I am undone; because I am a man of unclean lips, for mine eyes have seen the King, the Lord of hosts" (Isaiah vi:1-6). The lessons here, which the Seraphim give to us, we must not pass by.

The covering of their faces denotes their deep reverence. The higher a being is in creation the greater is the reverence given to the Creator-God. The Seraphim are nearest the throne hence their great reverence. And reverence, in its fullest expression, as it beholds the infinite One, is worship. They teach us reverence. Many years ago, Canon Liddon, an able and pious scholar, declared that "reverence is not one of the most popular virtues at the present time." It is much more true today. The lack of reverence, especially among the young, is appalling. Here, too, we must charge that vile offspring of the destructive criticism, Modernism, with being responsible for the deplorable irreverence of our times. "Where angels fear to tread, fools rush in." It is folly for the finite mind to sit in judgment upon God's holy infallible Word, to reject portions of it under the plea of human learning and scholarship, when the angels, with their superior knowledge, desire to look into these things. The destruction of the authority of the Word of God, as it has been going on in the camp of Modernism, not only robs man of faith, but it destroys the virtue of reverence. Evil days are in store for this age. Days of apostasy, ending with judgment, loom up on all sides. And what shall we say when even believers, certain evangelists, drag down "that worthy Name," and use it with an obnoxious familiarity. The Holy Spirit is the Spirit of reverence and worship. He never leads to anything but the deepest reverence. The more we know God and His only Son our Lord, the greater our reverence and worship.

The Seraphim also covered their feet. It means, symbolically, their humility. In covering their feet they acknowledge their own unworthiness. The last mentioned is, "with twain he did fly." This stands for service. They execute promptly and swiftly His commands. It is the very last, showing that service is not the first thing God wants. Reverence and worship is what God delights in. The Son of God has given us also the same truth. "God is a Spirit, and they that worship him must worship him in spirit and in truth." Before He uttered these words He said, "the Father seeketh such to worship him" (John iv:23, 24). True service for Him must be born in reverence and worship and must be coupled with humility, the deepest feeling of our unworthiness, that after all we are but unprofitable servants.

Bishop Bull (1634-1710) wrote about these lessons which come to us from the reverence, the worship, the humility and the service of the Seraphim and all the angels of God.

"When we consider what glorious beings the angels are, and yet that they are but creatures of, and servants to, the God whom we serve, waiting before His Throne, and humbly attending His commands; this consideration, if we let it sink deeply into our hearts, must needs possess us with most awful apprehensions of the glorious majesty of our God at all times, but especially in our approaches to Him in His worship, and fill us with the greatest reverence and humility. We should do well often to call to mind Daniel's vision, to whom was represented the 'Ancient of Days sitting upon His throne, a thousand thousand ministering unto Him, and ten thousand times ten thousand standing before Him.'

"With what reverence should we behave ourselves in our addresses to the Divine Majesty, before whom the Seraphim themselves hide their faces! And if they cover their feet, are conscious to themselves of their natural imperfection, compared to the infinitely glorious God; how should we clods of earth, we vile sinners, blush and be ashamed in His presence, assuming no confidence to ourselves, but what is founded on the mercies of God and the merits of our blessed Redeemer and Advocate, Jesus Christ!

"And when we find ourselves inclined to pride and vanity, to think highly of ourselves and of our services to God, let us reflect at what a vast distance we come behind the holy angels; how far short our poor, lame, imperfect services are of their holy and excellent ministry. Yet, when we think of the ministry which the holy angels perform towards God, and for us; let us at the same time propound them to ourselves, as patterns and examples for our imitation."

The Cherubim are another class of mighty beings close to the throne of God in worship and in government. We first meet them in the Bible as the sentinels of the garden of Eden, after man and the woman had been driven out. It was mercy which placed them there. For the tree of life was there and had man returned to eat of the tree of life, it would have resulted in a dreadful disaster for man. He would have lived forever, as to the *body*, and thus prolonged his miserable earth-existence, in sin, sickness, pain and sorrow on to endless being.*

Next we see them in connection with the mercy-seat (Exodus xxxvii:7, 9). They were there as beautiful figures of gold, as symbolical figures, their wings spread, covering the mercy seat, with their faces one to another. Their attitude is twofold, the attitude of worship and the attitude of deep contemplation. Here we may remember Peter's statement in the passage in which he speaks of the sufferings of Christ and the glory that should follow, and the Gospel, which is now preached, and then he adds, "which things the angels desire to look into" (1 Peter i:12). As they looked downward upon the mercy-seat, beholding, symbolically, the blood, they expressed the contemplative attitude of the angelic world, looking into the depths of that self-sacrificing love, which would be manifested in the gift of God's Son. Their figures also appeared embroidered on the curtains of the tabernacle (Ex. xxvi:1). Much else is connected with them in a symbolical way. We know from Ezekiel and from John's Patmos vision that their faces were fourfold—the lion, the ox, the man and the eagle. Israel journeyed through the wilderness in four

---

*It is an unscriptural invention to teach that man lost his immortality when he sinned. Immortality such as the breath of God imparted to man can never be lost.

As stated above, to live forever in Gen. iii:22 has nothing to do with the soul of man, but refers to the body.

great divisions, and each division had a banner. According to Jewish tradition, the standard of Judah had in it a lion; that of Reuben a human face. (Reuben means "Behold a son.") The division of Ephraim had the calf in the banner. In the banner of Dan was an eagle, the foe of the serpents. There is no valid reason to reject this rabbinical tradition. Symbolically these faces of the Cherubim represent the Son of God in His fourfold character—as King, represented by the lion; as Servant, represented by the ox; as Man, as the incarnate perfect Man; as the Eagle, which comes from the sky and swiftly mounts up, the emblem of the Son of God. This was known to the early church, for many ancient manuscripts associated the lion with the Gospel of Matthew, for it is the Gospel of the King. The Gospel of Mark, the record of His service, is symbolized by the ox; the Gospel of Luke, the record of the perfect Man, by the face of a man; and the Gospel of John, by the eagle.

Nineteen times the Cherubim are mentioned in the book of Ezekiel. This great Prophet-priest saw the visions of God in the prison colony by the River Chebar. In the first chapter of the book, which bears his name, is the detailed description of the glory of the Lord. He beheld the Schechinah cloud of glory and the chariot throne he beheld was surrounded and supported by the Cherubim. The greater portion of the vision concerns these mighty and mysterious creatures of God. In the midst of the glory cloud was seen the form of a Man; He is the Son of God anticipated as the incarnate One. The vision shows the very intimate relation of the Cherubim to the throne of God, to His government in righteousness and His judgments.* Later the prophet was transported to Jerusalem and saw the glory of the Lord departing from the temple and from the city. In his final vision, when he beheld the coming restoration, that glory with the Cherubim returns to fill that great house of worship, the millennial temple.

Nothing is seen of the Cherubim till we come to the book of consummation in the New Testament, the Revelation. To painstaking students of this book it is well known that not one of the visions of this great book, beginning with the fourth chapter, has been fulfilled. In that chapter we are introduced into heaven and the first thing we behold is the throne and He who occupies it. The twenty-four elders, sitting upon thrones, represent all the redeemed. Then in the midst of the throne and round about are the four Cherubim. The King James version uses the word "beast," but the right rendering is "living creatures," a term which disposes of the views of some that the Cherubim are not real beings. Like the Seraphim, they have six wings. Without a moment's rest they say, day and night: "Holy, holy, holy, Lord God Almighty, which was, and is, and is to come." We behold them again in the attitude of worship and praise in the fifth chapter. When the Lamb opens the first four seals of the book, each living creature says, "Come." In answer to their "Come," the four apocalyptic riders appear. The white-horse rider is the false Christ, who appears after the true Saints of God have left earth; the red-horse rider represents judgment by universal warfare; the black-horse rider, judgment by famine; and the pale-horse rider, judg-

---

*For the full explanation see an exposition of Ezekiel.

ment by pestilence. We learn from this that the Lord uses them in His future judgments. Their worship is also recorded in Revelation vii:11, while their connection with judgment is again stated in chapter xv:7. The last time they are mentioned is in Revelation xix:4, "And the four and twenty elders and the four living creatures fell down and worshipped God that sat on the throne, saying, Amen, Alleluia." What blessed things for us to believe now, and in holy anticipation to look forward to the day when we shall meet these great and glorious creatures of God face to face!

The heavenly hosts are also praising and adoring God. These

> "Wondrous beings who, ere the worlds were made,
> Millions of ages back, have stood around the
> Throne of God."

What glory must dwell in the highest heaven with its never-ceasing worship and adoration! How many things of which we, nor any mortal, have even dreamt of must go on there!

One of the interesting revelations in connection with angels is, what may be termed in human language, the court days in glory. The Book of Job, this most ancient book, contains the description of such days. It begins with the statement, "Now there was a day when the sons of God came to present themselves before the Lord, and Satan came also among them" (Job i:6). The story of Job is not an allegory, it is actual history. Nor is this court day an imagination, but reality. The sons of God are the angels. They gather at stated occasions before the throne. Among them Satan, the fallen Lucifer, appeared likewise.

He is forced to give an account of himself. His occupation is to walk as the restless spirit to and fro through the earth. Then, when the Lord speaks of Job, His servant, the dark shadow sneers and challenges God, accusing Job wrongfully, to permit him to attack the saint of God. What followed we read in the first chapter of Job. Not Satan triumphs, but the power and grace of God has in Job the victory. Another court day comes. The same scene is repeated. Once more the Lord puts Job into Satan's hand to touch his body, but not his life. The same result followed. Job did not sin and Satan must depart defeated in his purposes.

Satan is still the accuser of the brethren and perchance much of the severe suffering among the people of God may be traced to the same source. He accuses the children of God before God on account of their sins and failures. But Christ is there also, as the Advocate of His own. One of the night visions of Zechariah sheds interesting light on this (see Zechariah iii:1-5).

Some Christians think that Satan is cast out of heaven and has no longer any right of access to accuse before God. But the twelfth chapter of Revelation makes such a view impossible. The war between Michael and his angels and the dragon and the angels which belong to him, has not yet been fought. It is still future. When it will take place we shall see in another chapter. But when it comes, Satan will be cast out and the heavens rejoice, because the accuser of the brethren, which accused them day and night, is cast down to the earth, and can no longer accuse.

Another court day in heaven is described by the prophet Micaiah in 1 Kings xxii:19-23, "I saw the Lord sitting on His throne, and all the host of heaven standing by Him on His right hand and on His left. And the Lord said, Who shall persuade Ahab, that he may go up and fall at Ramoth-gilead? And one said this manner, and another on that manner. And there came forth a spirit, and stood before the Lord, and said, I will persuade him. And the Lord said unto him, Wherewith? And he said, I will go forth, and I will be a lying spirit in the mouth of all his prophets. And he said, Thou shalt persuade him, and prevail also, go forth and do so." Without explaining the meaning of this incident we use it only as an argument that there are certain days in glory when the hosts of heaven gather before the throne of God.

CHAPTER VII

More about Angels in the New Testament than in the Old.—Angels not omniscient.—1 Peter i:12.—Their deep interest in redemption.—The great conflict.—The opposing forces.—The Angels in Sodom.—Abraham and Eliezer.—Jacob and the Angels at Mahanaim.—The Law ordained by Angels.—Angelic protection.—Daniel's companions, and Daniel in the Lion's den.—Watching and waiting for redemption.

FROM heaven we turn to earth to examine the relation which the angels sustain to the earth and the human race. What is their service under God? It is a very interesting fact that much more is said about angels in the New Testament than in the Old Testament Scriptures. In the New Testament, the angels are the most frequently mentioned in the beginning of the New Testament Scriptures, that is, in the Gospels, and at the close, in the Book of Revelation. This in itself is of deep meaning. We shall return to it. We quote once more 1 Peter i:12, "which things the angels desire to look into." Their chief interest seems to be in connection with the redemption of man and the earth, which God gave to His creatures. They watched with holy awe when God said (not to angels), as the triune God, "Let us make man in our image, after our own likeness, and let them have dominion over the fish of the sea, and over the fowl of the air, and over the cattle, and over all the earth, and over every creeping thing that creepeth upon the earth" (Gen. i:26). They watched God as He fashioned man's body out of the dust of the ground and, breathing into him, communicated to this creature immortality. What shouts of joy must have come from them when man, the crown of all the earth, stood before his Creator, made a little lower than themselves, the angels. Angels are not omniscient. The future is only known to them as the omniscient God is pleased to reveal it. With what horror, then, they must have watched when the serpent, Satan, whom they knew so well, sneaked up to the woman and the fatal conversation began. If angels can weep and demons laugh, when sin was born conceived by the liar and murderer from the beginning, angels must have wept in deepest agony, while the demon-world shouted for joy.

And now the history of redemption begins. There is to be enmity between the serpent and the woman, between the seed of the woman and the seed of the serpent. There is to appear the seed of the woman to crush the serpent's head; the heel of the seed of the woman is to be wounded. He who defeats the serpent and gains the victory is to suffer. Now, angels begin in their eager desire to look into these things, the things concerning Him who is to come, concerning His suffering and the glory to follow.

In the great conflict which began upon earth they have a definite part to perform. Satan and his angels are active. The prince of the power of the air opposes God's purposes in redemption. He has his seed among men, those who side with him. The angels of God on the Lord's side are God's agencies in defeating the devil and his hosts; He uses them in behalf of His people, in their protection, in carrying out His plans and eternal purposes.

How little of all this we know! Here and there the veil is lifted in sacred history and we get glimpses of the service of the angels. Perhaps on purpose but little has been revealed so that we might escape the snare of being over-occupied with angels and the unseen things, instead of the Lord of Glory.

We remind the reader that "the Angel of the Lord" cannot be considered in this connection, for the Angel of the Presence is, as we have shown in the third chapter, the Lord Himself.

Angels came to Sodom. They were the companions of the Lord, who tarried with His friend Abraham. Lot, poor worldly Lot, sat in the gate. He recognized the strange visitors and invited them to tarry with him. How reluctant they were to enter his house! When the vile mob gathered to assault Lot, the angels protected him and smote the assailants with blindness. In the morning of the fatal day when judgment was to wipe out the wicked cities, the angels hastened Lot and, while he lingered, they laid hold upon his hand, the hands of his wife and daughters and brought them forth without the city. It was their God-sent errand of mercy to save Lot.

Abraham believed in angels and their ministries, for, when he sent forth Eliezer to fetch a bride for Isaac, he said: "He shall send his angel before thee." When Jacob was a wanderer away from the homeland, angels must have been at his side and shielded him. Finally, when returning to the land of his fathers, the angels of God met him. He recognized them and said,

"This is God's host, and he called the name of that place *Mahanaim*." This name means "double camp," or "double host." He realized that his own host was surrounded by the host from above. These angels must have reminded him of the vision he had twenty years before when he saw the angels of God ascending and descending on the ladder (Gen. xxviii:12), by which he must have been assured of divine protection, as now he knew that God was with him, for His hosts were about him.

An angel sent by the Lord kept Israel. But here, again, we are sure it is not a created angel but *the angel*, Jehovah, in angelic form, for we read of him something which can only be true of God Himself. "Beware of him and obey his voice, provoke him not, for he will not pardon your transgressions, for my name is in him." But we may be sure the ministry of angels attended Israel in her march from Egypt to the land of promise. How they were used in keeping Israel and perhaps in supplying them miraculously with food, we do not know.

But we know that the law "was ordained by angels" (Gal. iii:19), that they received the law by the "disposition of angels" (Acts vii:53).

From Psalm lxviii:17, we learn that the display of glory was effected by the ministration of thousands of angels. They were much in evidence on holy Sinai. Witness to it is given in Deuteronomy xxxiii:2 where the Lord is seen coming with ten thousands of saints, the correct translation is, "holy ones"—angels.

In the Psalms, we read of angelic protection. In Psalm xxxiv:7 it is again the Angel of the Lord, but in Psalm xci:11 the angels are revealed. "For he shall give his angels charge over thee, to keep thee in all thy ways. They shall bear thee up in their hands, lest thou dash thy foot against a stone." The ninety-first Psalm is prophetic. While the preceding Psalm shows the first man in failure and death, the ninety-first Psalm gives a prophetic picture of the second Man. The Devil knew this for he quoted this passage when he had led our Lord on a pinnacle of the temple. But whenever the devil uses Scripture, he either adds to it or takes away from it.* In quoting the promise concerning angelic protection, he left out the words "to keep thee in all thy ways." Only in God's ways can we claim His presence and His care.

We know the companions of Daniel passed through the fire unhurt, because the same angel who was in the burning bush was with them in the fiery furnace, and that was again the Lord in angelic form; Nebuchadnezzar bears witness of it, when he said, "Lo, I see four men loose, walking in the midst of the fire, and they have no hurt; and the fourth is like the Son of God" (Dan. iii:25). It must have been the same angel who stopped the lions' mouths when the aged Daniel had been cast into the lions' den. Happy words which came from Daniel's lips after a night spent with lions, "My God hath sent his angel, and hath shut the lions' mouths, that they have not hurt me" (Daniel vi:22).

To these incidents that angels are used of God in ministries on earth, in compassing about His people,

---

*All cults and error systems either take away from the Word of God or add to it, the significant marks of the power which stands behind them. This is true of Christian Science, Russellism, Spiritism, Theosophy, Mormonism, Bahaism and a lot of smaller isms.

in their protection, we add another where angels are not mentioned, though angels are meant. When Elisha's servant saw the forces of the enemy, with horses and chariots, surrounding the city, he was stricken with fear. But the prophet comforted him saying, "Fear not! for they that be with us are more than they that be against us." Then the Man of God prayed. "Lord, I pray thee, open his eyes that he may see." The prayer was answered at once and the young man saw the mountain full of horses and chariots of fire round about Elisha. The host of angels, heaven's warriors were with His people. In all the battles Israel fought, when they trusted the Lord and depended on Him, the hosts of the Lord fought for them and gave them the victory.

Satan's agencies are active on earth. The head of the kingdom of darkness walks to and fro in the earth (Job i) and that for the purpose to devour (1 Peter v:8). But God has His own forces which are also walking through the earth. Zechariah, the prophet, saw a vast company of horses, led by the rider upon the red horse. The question of the prophet, "O, my Lord, what are these?", was answered by the man upon the red horse, "These are they whom the Lord hath sent to walk to and fro through the earth" (Zech. i:8-10). Angels must have been constantly in service during the many centuries of Israel's history, sent forth from the throne of God to carry out His plans and purposes.

In the book of Daniel they are also revealed as watchers (Dan. iv:13, 17 and 23).

And all through the four thousand years of preparation for the promised redemption, beginning with the first promise in Eden, they waited for the increasing revelation of God's wondrous redemption plans, always desiring to look into these things. As God revealed, they learned and understood. His love towards a lost world became known to them. They listened to the voice of prophecy as the Spirit of God unfolded the sufferings of Christ and the glory that should follow. They learned that He, whom they knew as God's Only Begotten Son would some day come to earth, born of the Virgin. That He would suffer as the rejected One. The story of redemption as written in the Old Testament filled them with wonder, as more and more they desired to look into these things. While believing Israelites on earth waited for the promise, the Lord's hosts, the innumerable company of angels, waited in the heavens, in their dwelling places, for the appointed time.

CHAPTER VIII

Another court day in heaven.—The 400 silent years.—
Zechariah and the Angel.—Gabriel sent to the
Virgin of Nazareth.—Joseph's vision of an Angel.—
Angels announce the birth of Christ.—Why Angels
are so prominent in the Gospels and the last book
of the Bible.—Joseph warned by an Angel.—
Ministering to Christ.—During His life.—The Angel
in Gethsemane.—The witnesses of His suffering
and at death.—Present at His resurrection and
ascension.

AT last the appointed time had come. Perhaps
there was another great court day in heaven,
greater than any court day before. The heavenly
hosts surrounded the throne and stood in holy awe
and deepest reverence as the hour came for Him to
lay His glory by and to take on the creature's form,
to be made a little lower than the angels. O wonder
of wonders! The Lord who had created them by
whom and for whom all things were made, whom they
adore and worship, is about to leave heaven to come to
earth to fulfill all the prophets of God had spoken.
What a day it must have been when God was about to
send forth His Son to become incarnate! Four
hundred years of silence had passed since Malachi
had delivered the last message, announcing once more
His coming and His day. Four hundred years the
Lord did not speak as He had spoken before, and no

angels had been manifested. We are aware that the
so-called *Apocryphae* contain numerous references to
angels, but it does not take much discernment to see
that they are spurious and of a far different nature to
the chaste and dignified accounts in the Word of God.*
These apocryphal books have been rejected as un-
inspired by the true church, while the Romish church
has endorsed them because they support their unscriptural doctrines and practices. At best the angelic
manifestations described in these writings are the
records of the superstitions of the centuries when God
did not speak. But now the silence is to be broken.

An aged priest, a righteous man, one of those who
trusted the Lord and waited in faith and patience for
the consolation of Israel, the coming of the Messiah,
was burning incense in the temple, while the multitude
stood outside. His name was Zechariah, which means
"the Lord remembers", and his aged wife was Elizabeth,
which means "God's oath". The time had come when
God would remember His oathbound covenants.
The couple had no child, because Elizabeth was
barren, and they both were well stricken in years
(Luke i:7). All at once, while Zechariah officiated,
there appeared at the right side of the altar an angel
of the Lord. The angel speaks; the silence is broken.
From the throne of God this angel carried the message
which announces the coming birth of him who is to
go before the incarnate Lord of glory, "in the spirit and

---

*For instance, in the Book of Tobit is an account of an angel
by name of Rafael. The young man whom the angel accompanied was in danger of being devoured by a big fish. The angel
saved him. Then he told the young man to use the heart and
liver of the fish against demon influences, and the gall against
eye diseases, etc. This is not revelation but a childish fairy
tale. Other stories are even more ridiculous.

power of Elias, to turn the hearts of the fathers to the children, and the disobedient to the wisdom of the just, to make ready a people prepared for the Lord" (Luke i:17).   A few months later a still greater message was given to Gabriel.   The same Gabriel, who was made to fly swiftly almost six centuries before to announce exactly when Christ should suffer (Dan. ix:24-27), is now sent from the heavenly court to the poor little city of Nazareth.   There dwelt the Virgin who, as Isaiah predicted, should bring forth a son, whose name should be Immanuel.   No greater news ever came from heaven to earth.   Well can we imagine the deep and solemn interest of the angelic world, as in holy anticipation they looked on, and gazed forward to the days of the Son of God on earth.

Like the angel who spoke to Zechariah, Gabriel also said, "Fear not!"   But his first words to Mary of Nazareth were words of blessed salutation.   "Hail, thou that art highly favoured, the Lord is with thee; blessed art thou among women."   The word "Hail" means literally "Oh joy!"   Then comes the great and blessed announcement, "Behold, thou shalt conceive in thy womb, and bring forth a son, and shalt call his name Jesus.   He shall be great, and shall be called the Son of the Highest; and the Lord God shall give unto him the throne of his father David; and he shall reign over the house of Jacob; and of his kingdom there shall be no end" (Luke i:31-33).   Once more the angel speaks in answer to her question, "How shall this be?" "And the angel answered and said unto her, The Holy Spirit shall come upon thee, and the power of the Highest shall overshadow thee; therefore also that holy thing which shall be born of thee shall be called the

Son of God" (Luke i:35). How very simple, yet how deep, beyond human ken this angelic statement! Gabriel himself must have uttered these blessed words in holy reverence. The angels had been the witnesses, when the triune God formed man out of the dust of the earth. The second man did not need to be created, for He is the Lord "whose goings forth have been from of old, from everlasting" (Micah v:2). He comes to take on the body of the first man and that body is called into existence by a creative act of the third person of the Holy Trinity. He Himself, the Highest, is going to overshadow the Virgin, to unite Himself with that body. Here is the great mystery over which the innumerable hosts of angels pondered in holy awe. What must be their feeling when they see man, the creature of the dust, for whom God sent His only begotten Son, with his darkened mind and unbelieving heart turning away from the mystery of Godliness (1 Tim. iii:16), and refusing to believe in Him whom the Father sent! It seems to us they must shudder and tremble when they listen to the denials of the Virgin birth, for which they waited, the denials so prominent in the religious world of today.

Joseph, to whom Mary, the Virgin, was espoused, had the visit of an angel of the Lord. He is a beautiful character, righteous and tender hearted. When Mary was found with child of the Holy Spirit, "then Joseph her husband, being a just man, and not willing to make her a public example, was minded to put her away privately. But while he thought on these things, an angel of the Lord appeared unto him in a dream, saying, Joseph, thou son of David, fear not to take unto thee Mary thy wife, for that which is conceived in her is of the Holy Spirit." He was obedient to the angel's command. "Then Joseph being raised from the sleep did as the angel of the Lord had bidden him, and took unto him his wife, and knew her not till she had brought forth her firstborn son, and he called his name Jesus" (Matt. i:18-25).

The memorable night had come. The long expected child is cradled in a manger in Bethlehem. The seed of the woman has come. All heaven was astir that night. The whole universe filled with the angels of God knows what has taken place. The earth alone is in ignorance of the great event. Shepherds in the field keeping watch over their flock by night were suddenly startled by the appearance of an angel of the Lord.* These shepherds belonged to the pious in Israel, waiting for the promised Redeemer-King. Perhaps that very night they were meditating on these things and praying, like all pious Jews had been praying, for the coming of the Son of David. The glory of the Lord shone about them and in the glory an angel, the messenger of God. No wonder that they were sore afraid. Then the angel delivered the message. "Fear not!" had been spoken to Zechariah and to Mary of Nazareth, and this angel also says, "Fear not! For behold I bring you good tidings of great joy, which shall be to all people. For unto you is born this day in the city of David a Saviour, which is Christ the Lord" (Luke ii:10, 11). Blessed news this messenger brought to earth for man to listen to and to believe! But while they had gazed into the glory light, they did

---

*Not "*the*" angel, but *an* angel. The Authorized Version is incorrect in using several times in the New Testament the definite article.

not realize that the angel had a multitude of companions. "And suddenly there was with the angel a multitude of the heavenly host praising God, and saying, Glory to God in the highest, and on earth peace, good will toward men." It must have been a vast host and their praise and joyful declaration was not only heard by the shepherds, but it extended upward and wherever the angels dwell the same praise probably sounded forth. The angelic hosts having watched for four thousand years the preparation for redemption, being used by the Lord in His service and in the conflicts on earth, listening all the while to the voice of prophecy, ever desiring to look into these things, had learned some of the secrets of God's love in redemption. They knew God would ultimately be glorified in the highest; that poor, suffering, blood-drenched earth, with its restless nations like the restless sea, would have peace, while the loving, gracious will of God toward lost man would now be fully revealed in Him who had come from heaven to earth.

We meet angels on the threshold of the New Testament. Angels are very prominent in the Gospel records. It could not be otherwise. He who had created the angels, whom they worshipped as Lord; He who would, after a few years, return in His glorified humanity to heaven, to receive a place higher than the angels, was now on earth made a little lower than the angels. Because He was here the angels were present and seen by human eyes, while He Himself was attended by the angels. And even after He had left the earth angels were still seen, in connection with the beginning of the church, the body of Christ, that great mystery, which was new to angels, for it had not been revealed in former ages.

In the last book of the Bible, the Book of Revelation, angels are still more prominent, for that book concerns mostly the coming of the Lord, His return to the earth. In that day the earth will become the scene of glory as never before in its history. Angels will then be manifested and be seen in their heavenly glory, the invisible things will become visible. That is the reason why angels are so prominent in the beginning of the New Testament and in the closing book.

The next manifestation of an angel, after the shepherds had seen the heavenly hosts, happened again to Joseph. Angels appear always to him in a dream. It was so when he had discovered that his Virgin-bride was with child. When Herod was getting ready to have the children in Bethlehem killed, "an angel of the Lord appeared unto Joseph in a dream, saying, Arise, take the young child and his mother, and flee into Egypt, and be thou there until I bring thee word, for Herod will seek the young child to destroy Him" (Matt. ii:13). It was Satan's attempt through Herod to kill the child. But he could not do it. That child was not like any other child, subject to disease and death. It was not an innocent child, but a holy child. No sin was in Him and where there is no sin death has no claim. Herod's rage against the child is used by God as an occasion to fulfill His own purpose. That child is the true Israel of God. Israel, the nation, in her youth was as the first born son called out of Egypt. Christ had to pass though the same history in a perfect way of perfect obedience without any failure. Herod could not touch the life of the child. He sought to destroy it, but no Roman soldier could have ever plunged the sword into His little breast. And when Herod was dead the angel appeared again to Joseph commanding him to return to the land of Israel.

Some of the old masters, in painting the flight to Egypt, associated with it an angel, or angels, accompanying the child, His mother and Joseph. These heavenly beings were surely about and around the infant. They kept their watch over Him. The Jews have an interesting tradition concerning Adam, the first man in his unfallen state. The tradition says that he had the angels for his servants, that he had power and authority to command them to minister to his need. Perhaps this is true. But we know it is true of the second man, the last Adam, our blessed Lord. Angels were His ministers. It has not pleased the Holy Spirit to give us a record of the years of His boyhood and youth, save the one incident of going to Jerusalem in His twelfth year. We doubt not angels were about Him all through these years.

The first time we find angels mentioned in His public life on earth is in the fourth chapter of Matthew. After His Sonship had been declared by the Father's voice at the banks of Jordan, He was led by the Spirit into the wilderness to be tested by the devil. As stated before, the devil quoted Scripture. He knew that the ninety-first psalm was written by the Spirit of God describing the second Man walking in obedience and trusting God on earth. He, the Son of God incarnate, dwelled in the secret place of the most High. He said to God, "My God, in him I will trust." And therefore the promise "He shall give his angels charge over thee, to keep thee in all thy ways. They shall bear thee up in their hands, lest thou dash thy foot against a stone," belonged to Him. Satan knew this and tried to make the Lord Jesus act in self-will. After He had spoken His majestic, "Get thee behind me Satan!" the Gospels tell us that angels appeared on the scene. "Then the devil leaveth him, and behold, angels came and ministered unto him" (Matt. iv:11). Mark gives us additional information, "He was there in the wilderness forty days, tempted of Satan; *and was with the wild beasts;* and angels ministered unto Him" (Mark i:13). We do not know in what the ministry of the angels consisted. We believe it must have concerned His physical needs. He was in a wilderness. The devil had asked Him, when He hungered, to turn stones into bread. He had the power to do it, but He would have acted, in doing this, to please Himself. And, now, after the victory was won and the devil had left Him, His physical needs were still unsupplied. Therefore, angels appeared to minister to Him. Though this is the only place in the Gospels in which we read that angels ministered to the Son of God on earth, besides in Gethsemane, there can be no question that they ministered to Him on many other occasions. They were the onlookers, the holy watchers above Him and around Him. If they are now, as we shall show later, the unseen witnesses when Christians worship (1 Cor. xi:10), how much more must they have seen and watched Him as He lived that blessed life on earth. There is one sentence which confirms this fact. Paul writes that He was "seen of angels" (1 Tim. iii:16). He was seen of angels in every period of His life on earth, in His sufferings, in His death, in His resurrection and in His ascension.

They beheld Him as He went about doing good. They watched His deeds of mercy and power, how He healed the sick and cleansed the lepers. They must have rejoiced when with His omnipotent power He drove out the demons and delivered their victims from possession. They listened to His words. They hovered about Him in the nights spent in mountain tops and in desert places, when He held communion with His Father and prayed. They were the silent witnesses of the plottings of His enemies. They must have grieved when men turned away from Him, and rejoiced when others fell at His blessed feet and worshipped Him.

What must have been the effect of His sufferings with these holy watchers? They knew that He came to earth to be the Lamb of God, to suffer and to die. They witnessed His agony in the garden and listened to His prayer, His strong crying and His tears. "And there appeared an angel unto him from heaven, strengthening him" (Luke xxii:43). Here, again, we are not told in what way he strengthened Him. Some have imagined that Satan was present and exercised such power that Christ feared He might succumb under it and, dying in the garden, might not be able to finish the work on the cross. But that is a theory which gives the devil a power over Christ, which he had not, besides being dishonoring to our Lord. The agony was not produced by Satan's power, but it was in the anticipation of the Holy One, who knew no sin, now to be made sin for us. His holy soul shrank from that. The angel may have carried a message from the Father to the Son. Gethsemane,

in its deep sorrow, is one of the mysteries connected
with His suffering.

Angels saw Him when He was mocked, cruelly
scourged and His face marred and dishonored. Legions
of angels hovered nearby and He might have asked
the Father and more than twelve legions of angels
would have appeared in His behalf (Matt. xxvi:53).
But when He spoke about the twelve legions of angels
to Peter, who had drawn the sword in His defense,
He adds, "But how, then, shall the Scriptures be fulfilled, that thus it must be?" The angels knew that
the Scriptures must be fulfilled, that His hands and
feet must be pierced, that He must be afflicted and
smitten of God. Surely they must have veiled their
faces as they beheld the shame of the cross which He
despised and the suffering He endured so patiently.
Then came the three hours of darkness. Was it con-
fined only to our solar system, or did it extend throughout all the heavens? All heaven must have been
affected by what was going on in that little land of
one of the smallest planets of the universe. Creation's
Lord died for the creature's sin! The Just and Holy
One died for the unjust! The deepest mystery of
His atoning work, the cry from the cross, "My God,
My God, why hast thou forsaken me?" was even for
angels shrouded in darkness, a darkness which they
could not pierce. But how they must have wondered
at God's great love as well as at His righteousness and
wisdom revealed in the cross of Christ!

The work was done. "It is finished!" was His
triumphant utterance. It was heard by those who
stood by. But angels heard it and perchance the

shout, "It is finished!" was passed on from star to star in the universe till all heaven vibrated with the glorious news, "It is finished! It is finished!"

"And behold, the veil of the temple was rent in twain from the top to the bottom." For all we know it may have been an angel whom God commissioned to make that rent so that it might be known at once that the new and living way into the Holiest, the very presence of God, had been made by His precious blood.

While Roman soldiers watched at the sealed tomb, there were other watchers. The dawn of the first day of the week was nearing, while Mary Magdalene and the other Mary approached the sepulchre, where He had been buried. "And, behold, there was a great earthquake, for an angel of the Lord descended from heaven, and came and rolled back the stone from the door and sat upon it. His countenance was like lightning and his raiment white as snow" (Matt. xxviii:2-3). The earthquake was occasioned by the descending angel, and the stone, so securely sealed, was rolled away by angelic power. However, the resurrection of the Lord did not take place when the stone was rolled away. No angel was needed nor angelic power to open for Him the way from the tomb. It was God who raised Him from among the dead; but equally true it is that He Himself arose. The stone was rolled away to show that the tomb was empty. With what heavenly joy that angel must have told out the good news to the two women. "Fear not ye; for I know that ye seek Jesus, who was crucified. He is not here; for He is risen, as He said. Come, see the place where the Lord lay. And go quickly, and tell His disciples that He is risen from among the dead; and,

behold he goeth before you into Galilee; there ye shall
see him; lo I have told you" (Matt. xxviii:5-8). And
Mark tells us: "And very early in the morning the
first day of the week, they (the women) came unto the
sepulchre at the rising of the sun. And they said
among themselves, Who shall roll us away the stone
from the door of the sepulchre? And when they
looked, they saw that the stone was rolled away, for
it was very great. And entering into the sepulchre
they saw a young man sitting on the right side, clothed
in a long white garment, and they were very affrighted"
(Mark xvi:2-5). Luke says, "They found the stone
rolled away from the sepulchre. And they entered in
and found not the body of the Lord Jesus. And it came
to pass, as they were much perplexed thereabout,
behold, two men stood by them in shining garments.
And as they were afraid, and bowed down their faces
to the earth, they said unto them, Why seek ye the
living among the dead? He is not here, but is risen.
Remember how he spake unto you when he was yet in
Galilee, saying, the Son of Man must be delivered into
the hands of sinful men, and be crucified, and the third
day rise again" (Luke xxiv:2-7). And John tells of
these angels. "But Mary stood without at the
sepulchre weeping, and as she wept, she stooped down,
and looked into the sepulchre and seeth two angels in
white sitting, the one at the head, and the other at the
feet, where the body of Jesus had lain. And they say
unto her, Woman why weepest thou?" (John xx:
11:13).* He was seen of angels in His resurrection.
They were the messengers at the empty tomb telling
out the blessed news that He is risen, as they told out

---

*There is no discrepancy in these different accounts.

the story of His birth. They also manifested loving sympathy for His perplexed disciples. From all this we learn of their intimate connection with the life and work of our ever blessed and adorable Lord.

They were present when He ascended on high. The cloud had received Him out of their sight. "And while they looked steadfastly toward heaven as he went up, behold, two men stood by them in white apparel, which also said, Ye men of Galilee, why stand ye gazing up into heaven? This same Jesus, which is taken up from you into heaven, shall so come in like manner as ye have seen him go into heaven" (Acts i:10, 11). There is a theory taught by some that these two were Moses and Elijah. We do not believe this is true; the two in white apparel were angels.

"Seen of angels" is true, likewise, of His glorious ascension, when He passed through the heavens, as the glorified man, the mighty victor over sin, death and the grave. It must have been a great triumphal train, headed by Himself and followed by the angelic hosts. We believe there is a strong hint about this in the sixty-eighth psalm. "The chariots of God are twenty thousand, even thousands of angels, the Lord is among them as in Sinai in the holy place. Thou hast ascended on high, thou hast led captivity captive, thou hast received gifts for men, yea for the rebellious also, that the Lord God might dwell among them" (Psalm lxviii:17, 18). Before we follow the risen and glorified Man to His place of exaltation and describe how He is made so much better than the angels, we devote a chapter to the words spoken by our Lord concerning the angels and their activities.

CHAPTER IX

The denial of Modernism.—Christ's testimony concerning Angels.—As to their corporality.—Their
interest in the earth.—Rejoicing over repenting
sinners.—Lazarus and the Angels.—In connection
with His second coming.—In the kingdom parables
described as reapers.—Present at the judgment
throne.—The meaning of Matthew xviii:10.

AS we have stated before, the infidelity of Modernism and the destructive criticism, both denying
the existence of angels, is answered conclusively by our
Lord. He spoke a number of times of the angels and
associated them frequently with His own glory. To
deny the existence of angels charges the Lord Jesus
Christ with having taught something which is not
true. Such a denial makes of Him a fallible teacher
and strikes at His Deity. We give a brief review of the
different passages in the four Gospels in which our
Lord mentions the angels.

I. As to their existence and corporality. "They
which shall be accounted worthy to obtain that world,
and the resurrection from among the dead, neither
marry, nor are given in marriage, neither can they die
any more; for they are equal unto the angels; and are
the children of God, being the children of the resurrection" (Luke xx:35, 36; Matt. xxii:30; Mark
xii:25). If there were no angels these words of our
Lord would be a deception. But His witness is true

for He came from heaven and knows the angels, for He is their Creator. As pointed out before, this passage teaches the corporality of the angels.

II. As to their presence on earth. "Likewise I say unto you, there is joy in the presence of the angels of God over one sinner that repenteth" (Luke xv:10). They are in close touch with what is going on in the earth and when one sinner repents and turns to the Lord there is great rejoicing among them.

They are active in connection with the departure of believers out of this life. "And it came to pass, that the beggar died, and was carried by the angels to Abraham's bosom" (Luke xvi:22). Not a few expositors say that the story of Dives and Lazarus is only a parable. Our Lord did not say so. He said: "There was a certain rich man, which was clothed in purple and fine linen, and fared sumptuously every day; and there was a certain beggar named Lazarus, which was laid at his gate, full of sores." If it had been a parable the Spirit of God would have stated it, but the Lord spoke of the actual existence of that rich man and the beggar named Lazarus. The dispensational allegory, as given by the late Dr. Bullinger, is extremely fanciful. Our Lord gives us in this story the information that angels are used to carry the disembodied parts of believers to heaven.

III. When our Lord spoke as Prophet, revealing the future, His second coming, the judgments He will execute, the restoration of Israel, His own glory and His kingdom, He always mentioned the angels. As chapter xii deals exclusively with the future glory and the manifestation of angels and their ministries during the coming age of the kingdom, we give only the passages in which the Lord speaks of these things.

He speaks of the angels in His kingdom parables in the thirteenth chapter of Matthew. The end of the age brings the harvest and then angels will be used by Him. "The reapers are the angels" (verse 39). "The Son of Man shall send forth his angels, and they shall gather out of his kingdom all things that offend, and them which do iniquity" (Verse 41). "So shall it be at the end of the age, the angels shall come forth and shall sever the wicked from the just" (Verse 49). They will be used in gathering the elect. "And he shall send his angels with a great sound of a trumpet, and they shall gather together his elect from the four winds, from one end of heaven to the other" (Matt. xxiv:31). The elect are the people Israel and not the church as so many teach.

They will accompany Him in His second, visible and glorious coming. "For the Son of Man shall come in the glory of his Father with his angels, and then shall he reward every man according to his work" (Matt. xvi:27). They will be present before His judgment-seat. "Also I say unto you, Whosoever shall confess me before men, him shall the Son of Man also confess before the angels of God. But he that denieth me before men shall be denied before the angels of God" (Luke xii:8, 9).

As to the time of His second coming, the angels of God are ignorant of it. It is not known to them. "But of that day and that hour knoweth no man, no, not the angels which are in heaven, neither the Son, but the Father. Take ye heed, watch and pray, for

ye know not when the time is" (Mark xiii:32, 33).
What presumption, then, for man to try to figure out
the year and the time of that coming event!

Angels will be visibly seen in connection with the
throne of our Lord, the King of Israel. "Verily, verily
I say unto you, Afterward ye shall see heaven open,
and the angels of God ascending and descending upon
the Son of Man" (John i:51). Nathaniel had confessed
Him as the Son of God, the King of Israel. Then the
Lord promised him "greater things," which will come
when He is enthroned as King, when the invisible
angelic hosts will be seen by human eyes.

There is another passage in which our Lord mentions
the angels which we have not yet quoted. It is explained in different ways. "Take heed that ye despise
not one of these little ones; for I say unto you, that in
heaven their angels behold the face of my Father who
is in heaven" (Matt. xviii:10). It has been explained
as meaning that every believer has a guardian angel in
heaven. This we do not believe is the correct interpretation. He evidently speaks of the little children,
and not of believers. All depends of the interpretation
of the word "angels." At the first glance it would
seem as if these little ones have angels in heaven. There
is a passage in the twelfth chapter of Acts which seems
to solve this difficult passage. When Peter, rescued
from prison, by angelic interference, came to the house
where a prayer meeting was in progress and the maid
Rhoda maintained that Peter was knocking at the
door, they said, "It is his angel." They thought that
Peter had been killed and when they used the expression "his angel" they meant his disembodied spirit.
It throws some light on the passage before us. The

little children belong to the kingdom of heaven. When they depart in their infancy out of this life, their disembodied spirits behold the face of the Father in heaven. In other words, they are saved. These little ones perish not. The work of the Lord Jesus Christ brings them to glory. This seems to be the most satisfactory explanation of this passage.

Finally we do not overlook the angel who came at certain times to the pool Bethesda, agitating the waters so that healing powers were imparted (John v:1-9). Many critics attack this record and question its genuineness. "After all, there is no more real difficulty in this account than in the history of our Lord's temptation in the wilderness, the various cases of demon possession, or the release of Peter from prison by an angel. Once admit the existence of angels, their ministry on earth, and the possibility of their interposition to carry out God's designs, and there is nothing that ought to stumble us in this passage."

CHAPTER X

The great day of His return to heaven.—At the right hand of God in glorious exaltation.—The Lord Jesus Christ present in heaven in His glorious humanity.—A real body.—The great vision for Angels.—The marvellous redemption.—Man taken in redemption above the Angels.—Shares His glory. —The testimony of Hebrews i.

WHAT a day it must have been in glory when the Son of God, clothed in a real human body, returned to heaven, His eternal dwelling place! As we have stated before, angels accompanied Him in His glorious upward sweep, clothed in the Schechinah cloud. He passed through the heavens. All laws of nature, which He made and maintains in His creation, were set aside. Neither space nor time are anything with Him. He passed through the first heaven, passing the planets of our solar system, then He passed the distant constellations, way beyond the milky way, with its millions of suns, till the limit of the second heaven was reached. And there is the portal which leads into the third heaven, the heaven of heavens, which no human eye has ever seen. He advanced to enter in, surrounded by the worshipping hosts of angels. What a day it was when He left heaven to come down to earth! But it was a greater day when He returned, His work finished, to receive the place of honor and glory at the right hand of God. What shouts of glory must have then been heard! A mighty hallelujah chorus swept through the heavens as He seated Himself "at his own right hand in the heavenly places, far above all principality, and power, and might, and dominion, and every name that is named, not only in this world, but also in that which is to come" (Eph. i:20, 21). As He took that place, the once thorn-crowned Man, now crowned with glory and honor, angels and authorities and powers were made subject unto Him (1 Peter iii:22).

Seated, now, upon the throne of God, His God and our God, His Father and our Father, is the Man— Christ Jesus. The Lord Jesus has taken His incarnation body into heaven and in that glorified human body fills the highest place in glory. It is the same body which was created for Him in the Virgin's womb by the Holy Spirit. It is the body in which He lived on earth, toiled for man, in which He glorified God. It is the body, the sinless, the deathless body, which He gave as the mighty sacrifice on Calvary's cross. It is the body in which He suffered agony and shame, the body which passed through death on account of our sins. It is the body which was buried, but which could not see corruption. It is the body which was raised from among the dead and in which He ascended up on high. Oh blessed, blessed sight for faith to see Him there, the Man in the glory!

What a deep and blessed meaning it has! Man was made a little lower than the angels. Angels watched as the triune God carried out His purpose of eternity to have such a creature as man to inherit the earth. They saw that creature formed out of the dust of the earth with the divine breath, immortality communicated to him. Then came the awful catastrophe. Man, the offspring of God, falls into sin through the agency of the first sinner, Satan, the enemy of God. His inheritance is lost. The erstwhile owner of this earth becomes once more the prince and the god of this world. Man himself is dragged down and through sin becomes a subject to the power of darkness. The devil is man's master. He has fallen into a horrible depth. How is God to save His fallen creature? As we have seen, angels desired to look into these things and as God begins to reveal His purposes in redemption, they learn to know His plans. They know that the Son of God will be the Redeemer. He came, garbed as a servant in a human body and finished the great work the Father gave Him to do. And now He is back in glory and the form of man has been taken by Him into the highest heaven, to the nearest and dearest place in God's presence.

And, now, angels learn God's marvellous purposes in redemption. They begin to understand what God is accomplishing in the riches of His grace for lost sinners, redeemed by the blood of His own Son. They begin to see that He is but God's First Begotten Son in resurrection, and that sinners saved by grace are destined to be like Him, sharers of His nature, sharers of His place and sharers of His glory. They begin to see that His prayer request is answered, that the glory the Father gave to Him, He bestows upon His own (John xvii:21). They learn that every redeemed one will some day be with Him where He is, in the Father's house, and to inherit all things, as the heir of God and the joint heir of Jesus Christ. They understand that the Son of God will bring many sons unto glory and that ultimately Christ and His body, the Bridegroom and the bride will be at home in everlasting glory in the New Jerusalem.

What a wonderful redemption made known to lost sinners and also to the angels of God!   The redemption which does more than wash sins away, save from eternal night and give peace in time and eternity, the redemption which lifts man from where he is by nature as a fallen being and gives to him a place in Christ and a glory higher and better than the angels. Believers are made in redemption higher than the angels, for no angel can say to God, Father; nor is an angel indwelt by the Holy Spirit, nor is an angel an heir of God.

Angels behold now these marvels of redemption. They have found out what riches of glory are in store for those whom He purchased by the blood of His only Son. Poets have sometimes sung of angels envying. Angels know no envy; they cannot be jealous. Every new manifestation of the grace of God towards lost sinners, every new revelation of the surpassing riches of His grace in lifting man redeemed to the heights of Him who redeemed, brings forth from all the angels of God nothing but praise and ceaseless adoration. The evidence of this is found in the fifth chapter of Revelation. When the redeemed sing their song, "Thou art worthy to take the book, and to open the seals thereof, for thou wast slain, and hast redeemed us to God by thy blood out of every kindred, and tongue, and people, and nation; and hast made us unto our God kings and priests, and we shall reign over the earth," the myriads of angels join in the praise. "And I beheld, and I heard the voice of many angels round about the throne and the living creatures and the elders, and the number of them was ten thousand times ten thousand, and thousands of thousands, saying with a loud voice, Worthy is the Lamb that was slain to receive power, and riches, and wisdom, and strength, and honour, and glory, and blessing."

The first chapter in the Epistle to the Hebrews makes special mention of this most blessed phase of the Gospel. In a few sentences the Holy Spirit gives the facts concerning Christ, His person and His work. His Deity is stated in these words, "By whom he made the worlds, who being the brightness of his glory, and the express image of his person, and upholding all things by the word of his power." Then we read of His work in incarnation, "He made purification of our sins," and finally we have a statement of His resurrection glory: "Whom he hath appointed heir of all things * * * and he sat down on the right hand of the majesty on high."

In the fourth verse of this chapter angels are mentioned. "Being made so much better than the angels, as He hath by inheritance obtained a more excellent name than they." The Spirit of God uses next the witness of the psalms as to this exaltation. The second psalm is quoted. "For unto which of the angels said he at any time, Thou art my Son, this day have I begotten thee?" Nowhere is this spoken of angels, only He is Son incarnate and Son of God by resurrection from among the dead. In the eighty-ninth psalm God says that He would be to Him a Father— "I will be to Him a Father, and He shall be to Me a Son"; He never addressed such words to angels, but only to Him who is our Saviour. "And again, when he bringeth in the Firstbegotten into the world, he saith, and let all the angels of God worship him" (Psalm xcvii). The blessed meaning of angels worshipping the Christ is explained in our last chapter. But what are angels? They are spirits and a flame of fire, as His ministers (Psalm civ). But He is more than a servant. He has a throne and a sceptre in His kingdom (Psalm xlv). The One Hundred and Second Psalm speaks of that which could never be true of angels and the One Hundred and Tenth Psalm reveals, prophetically, the place which is His now in glory. "Sit on my right hand until I make thine enemies thy footstool." Never did God speak thus to an angel. No angel can sit in the presence of God. "Are they not all ministering spirits, sent forth to minister for them who shall be heirs of salvation?"

The truth that our Lord Jesus Christ is higher than the angels, and that we share in Him this place and are destined to share the glory He has, is a great, separating truth, if it is held in real heart occupation. Alas! there are only too many believers who believe it theoretically, but they never permit the power of it to control their lives and their daily walk. May the Holy Spirit of God make it a real power in the life of every one of our readers. When we realize in faith our unspeakable dignity, our marvellous calling and glorious destiny, a destiny far above all the angels of God, we shall walk in separation from this present evil age and demonstrate in our lives that which His blessed lips have spoken of us, "we are not of the world even as He is not of the world." But what will it be when some blessed day we shall be lifted by His power to the place where He is, to meet Him and the angels of God!

CHAPTER XI

The Book of Acts.—Opening chapters in Jerusalem.—
Why miracles and supernatural manifestations?—
Jews require a sign.—Angels also still visibly
present.—Apostles delivered by Angels.—Used in
judgment.—Philip guided by an Angel.—Cornelius
sees an Angel.—Paul's experience.—Angels no
longer visible in this age and why it is so.—They are
still active on earth.—Ephesians iii:8-11.—Present
in worship.—1 Corinthians xi:10.—How they are
now the ministering spirits for the Saints.—Practical
value of this truth.

THE Book of Acts contains the inspired record of
the beginning of the church of God on earth.
The day of Pentecost marks her birth, for on that day
the Holy Spirit of God came to earth and baptized
the assembled believers into one body (1 Cor. xii:13).
The beginning of the church was made in Jerusalem and
all members of it were believing Jews. As the Lord
had commanded, "beginning in Jerusalem," so it
was done. Yet not even the mouthpiece of the
Spirit of God, the apostle Peter, knew on the day of
Pentecost that Gentiles were to be added to that body.
The opening chapters of the Book of Acts present a
transition period. We are still on Jewish ground and,
therefore, different things took place which later,
when the Gospel is carried far hence to the Gentiles,
disappear. What happened in those apostolic days

in Jerusalem can never be repeated. How much confusion and error would have been avoided in the past, and especially in our days, if this were correctly understood. Such unscriptural movements as Pentecostalism, Dowieism and others, with their spurious claims of a restoration of apostolic gifts, especially the gift of talking in a strange tongue and the gift of healing, would not flourish if it had been understood that the supernatural manifestations recorded in the opening chapters of Acts had a special significance on account of the Jews. It is written, "the Jews require a sign" (1 Cor. i:22). It was so from the very beginning. It was only after Moses did the signs in the sight of the people, after his return from Midian, that the people believed (Ex. iv:29-31). God, in His loving kindness, met this demand "bearing witness, both with signs and wonders, and divers miracles, and gifts of the Holy Spirit, according to His own will" (Heb. ii:4). But these signs and miracles, so much needed in the beginning of this age, in behalf of the Jews, are no longer necessary after God's fullest revelation has been given. The age becomes the age of faith for "we live by faith and not by sight."

But in connection with the Jews and God's repeated offer of mercy, supernatural demonstrations were given. A lame man is supernaturally healed, signs and wonders were wrought by the apostles among the people. Multitudes came from the surrounding cities, bringing sick folks, and them which were vexed with unclean spirits; and they were healed every one. What the Lord Jesus had done was done by His apostles who used His Name, so that the unbelieving Jews might know that He whom they crucified is living and is their promised Messiah-King. There was also a supernatural judgment when Ananias and his wife Sapphira had told an untruth. Those who seek restoration of apostolic signs never mention this miracle of judgment. Furthermore, angels also are seen and act as God's messengers.

When the apostles were in the common prison, there was a miraculous deliverance. "An angel of the Lord by night opened the prison doors, and brought them forth, and said, Go, stand and speak in the temple to the people all the words of this life" (Acts v:17-20). It was an angel who gave direction to the evangelist Philip telling him where to go. "And an angel of the Lord spake unto Philip, saying, Arise, and go towards the South unto the way that goeth down from Jerusalem unto Gaza, which is desert" (Acts vii:26). And Philip obeyed without a moment's hesitation. It was an angel who appeared to Cornelius, the pious Centurion of the band called Italian, an earnest seeker after God. And the angel said to him, "Thy prayers and thine alms are come up for a memorial before God. And now send men to Joppa, and call for one Simon, whose surname is Peter. He lodgeth with one Simon the tanner, whose house is by the seaside, he shall tell thee what thou oughtest to do" (Acts x:3-6). God did not send this angel to preach the way of salvation to Cornelius, for this is not the calling of an angel, but to give direction to the Centurion of Cesarea.

In the twelfth chapter of Acts, Peter is in prison. Herod intended to kill him as he had killed James, with the sword. The church made prayer for Peter without ceasing. Their prayers were answered by a miracle. Peter was specially guarded, sleeping between two soldiers, bound with two chains, and the keepers before the door kept the prison. "And behold an angel of the Lord came upon him, and a light shined in the prison; and he smote Peter on the side, and raised him up, saying, Arise quickly. And his chains fell off his hands. And the angel said unto him, Gird thyself, and bind on thy sandals. And so he did. And he saith unto him, Cast thy garment about thee, and follow me. And he went out and followed him, and wist not that it was true which was done by the angel, but thought he saw a vision. When they were past the first and second ward, they came unto the iron gate that leadeth unto the city, which opened to them of its own accord, and they went out, and passed on through one street; and forthwith the angel departed from him" (xii:7-10). Evidently the two soldiers saw nothing and heard nothing of all this. Not even the chains which fell off to the floor awakened them out of their sleep. And even Peter did not realize that it was an angel; he felt as if it were a dream vision.

In the same chapter an angel is used in executing judgment upon wicked Herod, "Upon a set day Herod, arrayed in royal apparel, sat upon his throne, and made an oration unto them. And the people gave a shout, saying, It is the voice of a god, and not of a man. And immediately an angel of the Lord smote him, because he gave not the glory to God, and he was eaten of worms, and gave us the ghost."

The last time an angel is mentioned in the Book of Acts is in connection with Paul's journey to Rome. The prisoner of the Lord, when disaster stared the sea-faring company in the face, addressed them in the following words: "And now I exhort you to be of good cheer, for there shall be no loss of any man's life among you, but of the ship. For there stood by me this night an angel of God, whose I am, and whom I serve, Saying, fear not, Paul, thou must be brought before Caesar, and lo, God has given thee all them that sail with thee" (xxvii:22-27). In the last chapter of this book we see the great apostle Paul in a Roman prison. No angel appeared to open his prison door. And when later he is condemned to die, no angel comes to arrest the arm of the executioner. Throughout this age thousands upon thousands, tens of thousands, yea hundreds of thousands of Christians were cast into vile prisons, cruelly tortured and finally put to death in a merciless manner. No angels came to deliver them. The heavens are silent. Angels are no longer seen for the reason that God expects man to believe in His completed revelation.

But while no longer angels appear in visible form as in olden times as God's ministers, while these beings of the heavenly spheres no longer display their glorious figures, it does not mean in the least that they have ceased to visit the earth and are no longer active in the affairs of human existence. They are heaven's visitors still and He who has all power in heaven and on earth, who is far above the angels, uses them as His servants. There is Scripture evidence which makes this clear. It is true we lack a full revelation on the matter of the ministry of angels throughout this present age, and we will have to wait till all things become known to us in glory to find out the great and various services they rendered, under the Lord, to His people. There are also many traditions and legends from earliest times which claim that holy men and women were visited by angels. But no one can vouch for the genuineness of these things. Just as today in certain sects claims are made that they have seen angels in visions and in dreams.

In approaching, now, the present ministries of angels and their intercourse with the earth we quote first a passage from the Epistle to the Ephesians. In the third chapter of this epistle Paul speaks of his God-given ministry: "Unto me, who am less than the least of all the Saints, is this grace given, that I should preach among the Gentiles the unsearchable riches of Christ; and to make all men see what is the fellowship of the mystery, which from the beginning of the world hath been hid in God, who created all things by Jesus Christ; to the intent that now unto the principalities and powers in heavenly places might be made known by the church the manifold wisdom of God, according to the eternal purpose, which he purposed in Christ Jesus our Lord" (Eph. iii:8-11). The principalities and powers in the heavenly places are the angels. As we have seen, from the beginning the angels were desirous of looking into the things concerning redemption, the redemption of man. It was the great theme they followed in Old Testament times with wonder and adoration. When He came, the Saviour-Lord, they were intimately connected with His life and work on earth. But now they learn the manifold wisdom of God by the mystery of God which was hid in God from the beginning of the world. That mystery is the church. They see, now, that all who believe on the Lord Jesus Christ, Jews and Gentiles, become members of that body and that the Lord Jesus is the head of it. They see that in each heart dwells the Spirit of God, that they are one spirit with Him; that each member possesses His life, is of His flesh and of His bones (Eph. v:30). They behold how this building is fitly framed together, groweth towards its final destiny to be an holy temple unto the Lord. They watch to learn the manifold wisdom of God in all this so that the church, the body of Christ, the mystery made known, is, during this age, one of the great objects of angelic contemplation. If we, as believers, had this more real before our hearts, that these heavenly beings are watching and beholding us, how much more we would give all diligence to keep the unity of the Spirit in the bond of peace, and avoid everything which would mar in the least that unity. How angels must grieve when they see the degradation of the "church" and see those who are real members of the body of Christ divided amongst themselves. They know that such divisions are Christ–dishonoring and are not according to the purpose of God.

In the first epistle to the Corinthians, angels are mentioned in connection with the worship of the true church. We quote the verse: "For this cause ought the woman to have power on her head because of the angels." What is the meaning of this verse? God is the God of order not only in creation but also in redemption. Man and woman are given a place before Him. In the church, woman has her place given to her by the Lord. That place is revealed in 1 Timothy ii:11-14. "Let the women learn in silence with all subjection. But I suffer not a woman to teach, nor to usurp authority over the man, but to be in silence. For Adam was first formed, then Eve. And Adam was not deceived, but the woman being deceived was in the transgression." God has given to man the first place both in creation and in redemption. Woman takes her place as under the man. Paul, in this chapter, speaks of this when he writes by the Spirit of God that the head of the woman is the man; that the head of the man is Christ, and that the head of Christ is God. This is the scale of power ascending to the supreme God. Then he adds that the man was not created for the woman, but the woman for the man. In worship in the assembly, that is the church, woman has, therefore, her place which needs to be expressed outwardly. Man is to pray and worship with his head uncovered. He represents authority, and in this respect was invested with the glory of God, of whom he was the image. The woman is to have her head covered, as an outward sign and evidence that she is subject to the man; that covering is a token of the power to which she is subject. In connection with this the apostle speaks of the order in creation, according to which a woman's hair, her glory and attractive ornament, showed in contrast with the hair of the man, that she was not made to present herself before all with the boldness of man. "Given as a veil, her hair showed that modesty, submission (a covered head that hides itself, as it were, in that submission and in that modesty) was her true position, her distinctive glory."*

It hardly needs any mention how all these injunctions are ignored in our days. But few pay attention to them. Others say they are but unessential details and have no more meaning for us today. Sad it is to see how professedly Christian women can imitate the

*Synopsis J. N. D.

fashion of this world and have their hair shorn.   But
even these details are connected with the glory of the
Lord Jesus Christ.   We return to our theme.   The
woman, in her worship and in prayer, should cover her
head.   Besides maintaining the order of God she is
to do this because of the angels.   They look on while
the church is gathered to worship.   With what holy
admiration they must witness the supremest form of
worship on earth, when true believers gather around
the Lord's table to break the bread and partake of the
blessed cup, showing forth the Lord's death, till He
comes!   They behold the divine order then, man uncovered, the token of his place; woman with covered
head, the token of her place.   The verse teaches us
that angels behold the church in worship.   They are
the unseen witnesses when God's people meet in that
blessed and worthy name.

Another passage on the same truth we find in
1 Tim. v:21, "I charge thee before God, and the
Lord Jesus Christ, and the elect angels, that thou
observe these things without preferring one before
another, doing nothing by partiality."   Here, also it
is the question of order.   "Let all things be done
decently and in order" (1 Cor. xiv:40).   The elect
angels behold all these things.

We have already mentioned the words of our Lord
in the fifteenth chapter of Luke's Gospel, that there is
joy in the presence of the angels over one sinner that
repenteth.   They are looking on when the Gospel is
preached.   Unseen beings are present when the Holy
Spirit pleads with the unsaved to turn to Christ.
The demons are there to catch away the seed which

has been sown.   Angels watch and when one sinner repenteth they begin their rejoicing.

We learn then from these passages of Scripture that the church, the body and bride of the Lord Jesus Christ, is the special object of angelic occupation and contemplation.   Through the mystery of God hidden in former ages, they learn the manifold wisdom of God.   They look on when believers worship; they are the unseen witnesses when the Gospel is preached.

And now we turn to the verse in the New Testament which reveals the fact that angels are ministers of God during this dispensation.   "Are they not all ministering spirits, sent forth to minister for them who shall be heirs of salvation?" (Heb. i:4).   We take these words to mean exactly what they say.   The meaning is that the angels are ministering to those who shall be heirs of salvation.   There is a school of Bible interpretation which tries to rob believers of certain portions of the Word of God by saying that these portions are not for the church, but for the Jews.   This school claims the Gospels are mostly for the Jews.   The epistles of Peter, James and Hebrews are also Jewish; even the book of Revelation is Judaized.   They would have Christians read and study only certain epistles of the apostle Paul, addressed to the church.   A one-sided Bible study produces a one-sided character and a one-sided service.   And so they say because this verse is in Hebrews it has nothing to do with us.   They rob the church of a comfort which belongs to every child of God.   The fact that angels are ministering spirits sent forth from above is a neglected truth of the Word of God.   Rome's abuse in worshipping angels has kept evangelical Christians from examining more closely the ministry of angels.

As we think on this truth, it appears perfectly logical that angels minister to those who belong to Christ. They know that redeemed sinners, washed in the blood of the Lamb, are the glory of Christ. They know Christ dwells in them; they know that they are the heirs of salvation. As Christ was in the world so are they now in the world. They ministered to Christ and as the believers are in Christ's stead, sent into the world, as the Son of God was sent into the world (John xvii:18) they minister now to them. This appears so much more reasonable when we consider the hostile forces which are in the world. The world lieth in the wicked one. The devil is the god of this age, the prince of this world and the prince of the power in the air. He hates Christ. He tried to frustrate for four thousand years the purposes of God, and was active as the murderer and liar, to make it impossible for God to carry out His plans. And now that he is defeated and Christ is victor, seated as such at the right hand of God, he strikes at that which names the blessed Name of the Lord Jesus Christ on earth. His demon forces, through whom he acts, are active in every direction. If he could do it he would end the life of every child of God on earth. The true church is the object of his hatred. The angels of God are ministering to prevent the success of the devil's attacks.

But how do they minister? What kind of a ministry do they exercise? They cannot minister to believers in spiritual things. They cannot assist them in the study and in the understanding of the Word and the Truth of God. Believers have the unction from above, they are indwelt by the Holy Spirit. "But the anointing which ye have received of him abideth in you, and ye need not that any man teach you; but as the same anointing teacheth you of all things, and is truth, and is no lie, and even as it has taught you, ye shall abide in him" (1 John ii:27). "We have received, not the spirit of the world, but the Spirit which is of God; that we might know the things that are freely given to us of God. Which things we also speak, not in the words which man's wisdom teacheth, but which the Holy Spirit teacheth; comparing spiritual things with spiritual" (1 Cor. ii:12, 13). Angels are not the temples of the Holy Spirit, for the Spirit of God is the gift of the grace of God in the Lord Jesus Christ, given to those who believe on Him. Therefore, angels are beneath us in this respect and they cannot minister to us in spiritual things; God, the Holy Spirit, through the Word of God, of which He is the author, ministers to the spiritual needs of the flock of God.

In what, then, consist their ministries? In physical, temporal matters exclusively. In a world which is antagonistic to the children of God, which is controlled by the forces of evil, dangers and pitfalls abound on all sides. There are many perils. The apostle Paul had them in his life of service. "Of the Jews five times received I forty stripes but one. Thrice was I beaten with rods, once was I stoned, thrice I suffered shipwreck, a night and a day I have been in the deep. In journeyings often, in perils in water, in perils of robbers, in perils by my own countrymen, in perils by the heathen, in perils in the city, in perils in the wilderness, in perils in the sea, in perils among false brethren" (2 Cor. xi:24-26). We doubt not that all these perils were attempts made on his life. Satan used wicked men to beat him and to stone him. He used robbers and wild beasts (1 Cor. xv:32), his own countrymen and the heathen, to end his career, but the Lord saved him and kept him as long as his work was not finished. That angels were about him in these perils and were sent forth by the Lord to protect His faithful servant, ministering thus to him, in unquestionable. We have the hint of it in the story of the shipwreck, when an angel appeared to him, assuring him of his safety and that of the company which sailed with him.

The lives of the Lord's people are in the Lord's hands. It is a true saying, "We are immortal, as concerns the earth, as long as our work is not done." The Lord keeps the very feet of His saints and protects them in all perils and dangers. In this respect, life is full of mysteries. The great men of God in the past in every century record miraculous escapes from threatening dangers which they could not explain in any other way but by the ministry of the angels. We pray for heavenly protection; we put ourselves into His hands when we go on a journey; we commit our loved ones into His care and keeping. But how little we know how graciously our prayers and our trust in Him are answered in a supernatural manner by ministering angels! Children seem to be especially under the protecting care of the angels. Many miraculous escapes of little ones in the hour of danger can only be explained by supernatural agencies. When we remember the loving interest our Lord had in the little children when He was on earth, and His words, "Suffer the little children to come unto me, and forbid them not, for of such is the kingdom of heaven" (Matt. xix:14), we have a reason for the special watch and care of the angels over the little ones.

If we were to ask our fellow Christians to give us experiences of Providence, miraculous preservation and protection in the hours of danger, when death threatened, we would receive enough incidents to fill a volume. For years, the writer has watched in his own busy life of travel and service for Him, His gracious protection and many deliverances seem unexplainable apart from the services of unseen agencies. A number of years ago, while travelling northward, we committed ourselves especially into His loving hands. There was a feeling of danger in the heart. The Lord gave a night of peaceful rest. But in the morning we heard the story of what had happened during the night. The train was hours late and the crew told us that near to midnight the train had been flagged by a farmer and had been brought to a stop less than five yards from a deep abyss. A storm further north sent its flood-waters down the creek and washed the wooden bridge away. A farmer was asleep. He said a voice awoke him to arise. He heard the rushing water and hastily dressed himself and lit a lantern, when he heard the oncoming train, which he stopped in time. We have always believed that an angel of God acted then. And how many more incidents there are in all our lives. Simple faith can look up and thank the Lord for His kind providences, for His deliverances, for His protection and for the unknown and unseen ministers He uses in the execution of His purposes and the keeping of those who are "Beloved of God, called Saints." Surely the angels must compass those about who fear the Lord. It seems also that the words of Satan in the book of Job indicate this, when he said: "Hast thou not made a hedge about him, and about his house, and about all that he hath on all sides?"

Yet we cannot tell and we do not know all the ways in which this unseen ministry is done. We are assured that there is such a ministry and far be it from us to go beyond that which is written or to try to explore that which is God's secret. The story of Lazarus tells us how they are used when God's people die.

What other ministries the angels have in this great universe in connection with its government and its laws, we do not know. Bishop Westcott, the great scholar, wrote many years ago as follows: "We commonly limit our notion of angelic service to personal ministrations. No doubt Scripture dwells specially on this kind of office; but it indicates yet more, a ministration of angels in nature, which brings both them and the world closer to men. Perhaps one effect of the growing clearness with which we apprehend the laws of the physical phenomena is to bring out into prominence the thought of the powers which work according to them." "I can see," writes one who was himself a distinguished physiologist, "nothing in all nature but the loving acts of spiritual beings." But this is only a suggestion.

The day is coming when we shall no longer look into a glass darkly, when we shall know as we are known. Then we shall know these secret things and meet the angels. What discoveries we shall make then as we trace our little life's story in the light of God. Perhaps these blessed beings will tell us in glory of the many ways in which they were alongside of us, keeping and protecting, like a mighty shield, guarding and directing of which we never dreamt while clothed in a mortal body. Like every truth, the truth of the angels of God, their presence on earth and their loving ministries, has a practical value. As we realize in faith that we are the objects of observation of so many unseen beings, the host of angels, and, think of it, that they are watching us, ready to walk with us, as we walk with Him in His ways, ready to serve us as we serve Him, ready to shield us and help us in a hundred different ways, a solemn feeling will come into our lives. Surely we shall walk softly in the presence of the Lord and His holy angels. We shall remember that they also are witnesses of our deeds and listen to our words. Thus this truth will assist us in a holy life. Furthermore, as we remember that they are about us for our preservation and protection we can live for Him and serve Him without fearing the power of the enemy, knowing that our Lord will keep us in all His ways.

CHAPTER XII

The waiting heavens.—Christ waiting and Angels waiting.—His coming again and what it will mean.—
The visible manifestation.—1 Thess. iv:16-18.—
—Present at the Judgment seat.—Another great and
glorious court day in heaven.—Satan rebuked and
cast out.—Revelation and Angels used in judgment.
—The heavenly hosts manifested in the day of His
glory.—They are used by Him.—Hebrews i:6.—
The Angels ascending and descending. Conclusion.

THERE is waiting in Heaven. Once the heavens
were waiting when the Lord had spoken the first
prophecy and the first promise of redemption. The
waiting began with the third chapter in Genesis.
Angels waited for the accomplishment of God's
purposes in redemption, as we have shown in the
preceding chapters, desiring to look into these things,
and used by God as servants during the four thousand
years before He came as the promised seed of the
woman.

But the heavens are still waiting. The Christ as
the glorified Man, fills the throne in the highest heaven.
He is waiting till His enemies are made the footstool
of His feet, and that will be in the day when the
Father sends Him the second time, to claim His crown
rights over the earth, which He purchased by His blood.
The spirits of the redeemed are waiting for that coming
day when they will receive their resurrection bodies and

the rewards, and their crowns (2 Tim. iv:8). The innumerable company of angels are also waiting. On the earth the true church is waiting. The living members of His body, believers on every continent are longing for His coming and the long-forgotten prayer is now prayed as perhaps never before: "Even so, Come Lord Jesus."

Angels must, indeed, long with us for that promised day of consummation. We long for it because we know that day will bring His glory. When He appears in power and great glory every question which agitates the so-called "religious world" of today concerning His Person will be forever settled. Today, the men who call themselves "scholars," great "thinkers" or "scientists" sneer at the Virgin birth of our Lord, deny His miracles, because they are baptized infidels who do not believe in His Deity; they sneer at His resurrection and ridicule His return to earth. But when He comes again, when this same Jesus, in that same body which He had on earth and in which He is now at the right hand of God, reappears, the great scholars, thinkers and scientists, with their denials of Christ will be found miserable liars and put to shame. The curse of God will rest upon them, for it is written, "If any man love not the Lord Jesus Christ let him be anathema maranatha" (accursed when the Lord comes. 1 Cor. xvi:22).

Angels know all this and, therefore, they long with us for that day of His glory and victory. They also know that when the day of the Lord comes they will be manifested in their glory. The day will bring what they must long for, their visible display. Then modern Sadduceeism will be answered as the existence of angels is demonstrated in their glorious presence.

The Lord has been pleased to give to His people in His Word the order of events in connection with the end of this present age, His visible return, the dawn of the morning and the glories of the coming age. In all these events angels are very prominently mentioned in both Testaments.

It is well known to all painstaking Christians, who divide the Word of Truth rightly, that the Lord begins the events of the end of the age with the fulfillment of a promise which He did not give to the world, but only to His own. It is the familiar promise in John xiv, "I will come again and receive you unto myself that where I am ye may be also." He did not reveal at that time how this promise would be fulfilled. His disciples who listened to these words were Jews. They had never heard anything like it before. The hope of the Jew in the Old Testament was to be with the Messiah in His earthly kingdom and enjoy the kingdom blessings in Immanuel's land. The full revelation as to the manner of the fulfillment of this promise was given through the apostle Paul, who tells us that he received it by the Word of the Lord.

"For the Lord himself shall descend from heaven with a shout, with the voice of the archangel, with the trump of God, and the dead in Christ shall rise first; then we which are alive and remain shall be caught up together with them in clouds, to meet the Lord in the air, and so shall we ever be with the Lord" (1 Thess. iv:16-17). This is "that blessed Hope," the true hope of the church. We notice that in this great revelation the voice of the archangel is mentioned. The archangel is Michael. He is closely connected with the events in the end of the age (Daniel xii and Revelation xii). The Lord Himself comes as the Head of all things and gives the word. Then the archangel passes it on, and the trumpet of God will be sounded. Then comes the great and precious event. The righteous dead arise; the living believers are changed in a moment, in the twinkling of an eye, and all are caught up together in clouds to meet the Lord in the air.

The archangel Michael evidently represents as head of the angelic world the entire heavenly hosts. They will be onlookers when this great miracle takes place. Again, all heaven, it seems to us, will be astir, for here come the redeemed, the saints of God, the fellows of Christ, to receive His glory; and as it was with the forerunner so now again all laws of space, distances and time are not in operation as heaven's chariots carry the saints of God from earth to heaven. As He passed t hrough the heavens so the redeemed pass through the heavens. As He was seen of angels so angels see the fellow heirs of Christ in their glorious home-going. Then, too, the mysteries of the stars and the vast universe will be known by the future tenants of the heavens.

Angels will be witnesses at the judgment seat of Christ when the hidden things will be brought to light. When the rewards are given for faithful service and some will be approved and many others disapproved, when some receive crowns and others suffer loss, though saved as by fire. Angels will stand by, for they too watched the believers' works and witness for Christ (Luke xii:2, 3; 8, 9; 1 Cor. iii:11-15; iv:5).

It will be another marvellous court day in heaven, when all the redeemed are gathered before the throne.

The Sons of God, the angels, the Sons of Jehovah, the redeemed and glorified children of men are there, and, Satan will probably be there also. One of the night visions of Zechariah suggests this as a possibility (Zech. iii:1-4). In this vision Israel, the priestly nation is in view. It is equally true of the church; she too is "as a brand plucked out of the fire." Satan has been the accuser of the brethren. He tried his utmost to snatch away the members of His body, to pluck them out of His hand. The advocacy of Christ answered to all his malignant accusation. The complete body of Christ is now in glory; not a member is missing. His blessed words of assurance, teaching the eternal security of His own, given to Him by the Father, are realized (John x:28-29). The accuser of the brethren is now completely silenced. He cannot speak another word.

It is at that time when the impressive scene of the twelfth chapter of the Book of Revelation is enacted. The time has come when the accuser of the brethren is to be cast out of heaven. The true church, the Christ complete, He the Head, His church His Body, is in glory. There is war in heaven. The Lord calls to Michael, and the archangel summons his hosts to fight with the Dragon and with his angels. "And the great dragon was cast out, that old serpent called the Devil, and Satan, which deceiveth the whole world; he was cast out into the earth, and his angels were cast out with him. And I heard a loud voice saying in heaven, Now is come salvation, and strength, and the kingdom of our God, and the power of His Christ, for the accuser of our brethren is cast down, which accused them before God day and night" (Rev. xii:7-12). On the earth

Satan, the Devil, the Serpent called also the Dragon, will produce the great tribulation.

The great worship scenes which John beheld in Patmos, when the door was opened for him in heaven, and the voice commanded him to come up hither, will then be enacted (Rev. iv and v). The twenty-four elders, clothed in white raiment, seated upon thrones and wearing crowns, represent the redeemed. Then, when the Lord Jesus is about to manifest His kingly rights, the multitude of angels breaks forth in adoration and worship.

When the Lord Jesus Christ opens the seven-sealed book, He received from the hand of God, the book in which are written the judgments for this earth, the book He alone is worthy to open, the four Cherubim and the angels are seen in action. During the seven years between His coming for His Saints (1 Thess. iv:13-18) and His coming with His Saints, supernatural powers will be manifested on the earth. Satan is on the earth and the two beasts of Revelation xiii, energized by the Dragon, control the politics and the ecclesiastical affairs of apostate Christendom. Lying signs and miracles appear on all sides, the great delusion has come (2 Thess. ii). Angels, as the agents of judgment, reach into the affairs of the world. These judgments, the contents of the book our Lord received, are revealed in chapters vi-xix of the last book of the Bible. All is yet to come. Nothing has been fulfilled in these chapters, nor are they in process of fulfillment now. The Saints of God must first be brought to glory.

When the Lord begins His judgment work and breaks the first four seals, each one of the Cherubim says,

"Come," and in response the four apocalyptic riders appear. Angels are seen in the seventh chapter restraining the four winds of the earth, while another angel seals the 144,000, the remnant of Israel, turning to the Lord during that time of Jacob's trouble. Seven angels appear sounding their trumpets and after each sounding a judgment falls upon the earth.* In almost every chapter angels are mentioned, sufficient evidence that the Lord uses them in His judgments which fall then upon the earth. Six angels are prominent in the fourteenth chapter. One announces the everlasting Gospel; the second announces the fall of Babylon, and the third warns against worshipping the beast, the Anti-christ, and his image, and receiving the mark of the beast. The fourth angel comes out of the temple calling for the harvest of the earth, followed by the fifth angel who carried a sharp sickle. The sixth angel "cried with a loud cry to him that had the sharp sickle, saying, Thrust in thy sharp sickle, and gather the clusters of the vine of the earth; for the grapes are fully ripe." After that, seven other angels appear; they carried the vials filled with the wrath of God. Each pours out his vial and a judgment-plague falls upon the earth. One of these seven angels showed also to John the great mystical Babylon, Babylon the great, the mother of harlots and abominations on the earth, while another angel announces the complete fall of Babylon (Rev. xvii:1 and xviii:1).† From all this we learn how our Lord, to whom all judgment is committed, will use the angels in these future judgments of the earth.

*The word "angel" in Chapter viii should be "eagle."
†See the author's Exposition of Revelation.

At last the great day, called by the prophets the day of the Lord, has come. It is the day of which He so often spoke, "when the sign of the Son of Man shall appear in heaven," when the dwellers on the earth "shall see the Son of Man coming in the clouds of heaven with power and great glory." It is the glorious day when He comes in the glory of His Father with His angels, the day when the veil is lifted and the angels will be seen on a far greater scale than when He entered the world in Bethlehem.

The nineteenth chapter of Revelation gives us a great prophetic picture of that coming event. Heaven is once more astir, for now the time has come when He shall be revealed from heaven with His mighty angels, when He shall come bringing His own redeemed ones with Him. All heaven is in commotion. A great voice of much people in heaven shout their hallelujahs. "Hallelujah! Salvation, and glory, and honor and power unto the Lord our God." And after this vast multitude shouts again, "Hallelujah!" the twenty-four elders and the four living creatures, the Cherubim, fall down and worship saying, "Amen, Hallelujah!" Then comes the voice of a great multitude, which must be the innumerable company of angels, like the voice of many waters, as the voice of mighty thunderings, saying, "Hallelujah for the Lord God omnipotent reigneth." Heaven is filled with praise and joy, because everything is ready for the great manifestation, for which the ages waited. The Lamb's wife, the glorified church, is ready for the grand and glorious display. She is arrayed in fine linen, clean and white. The archangel Michael is ready as the chief commander of the heavenly hosts to do the part which belongs to him (Daniel xii). All the angelic hosts are ready, awaiting the word to take their places in the train of the King of kings and Lord of lords.

The spot to which the Lord Jesus Christ is to descend is His beloved Jerusalem, and over yonder in the East, the Mount of Olives. Jerusalem, in that day, is once more in a desperate condition. All nations are gathered together against her to battle. In the midst of the city is a faithful remnant crying to heaven for interference. "Oh that thou wouldest rend the heavens, that thou wouldest come down, that the mountains might flow down at thy presence" (Isaiah lxiv:1). They wait for the coming of the King. They know that the prophet Zechariah foresaw this very siege of Jerusalem; and they know what else must happen. For it is written, "Then shall the Lord go forth and fight against those nations, as when he fought in the day of battle. And his feet shall stand in that day upon the mount of Olives, * * * and the Lord my God shall come and all the holy ones (angels) with thee" (Zechariah xiv). And as they look upward to heaven there is suddenly a glory flash. The sign of the Son of Man appears. It must be the Schechinah cloud. As these believing Jews see it, they shout for joy, "Lo, this is our God, we have waited for him, and he will save us; this is the Lord, we have waited for him, we will be glad and rejoice in his salvation." A greater glory than the glory which shone around the shepherds the night Christ was born covers the heavens, a glory so great that the physical sun begins to darken, for the Sun of Righteousness is about to rise. Heaven is opened and the vision of the lone prisoner in Patmos becomes history (Rev. xix:11-16). The leader and center of all is the Son of Man, He who has a name written known only to Himself; whose name is the Word of God, whose name, written on His thigh, is King of kings and Lord of lords. With Him are the armies of heaven, the Saints of God, clad all in white. The closest to Him is His beloved bride and His body, the Church, and close to the Church, the friends of the bridegroom, the Old Testament Saints. Then the multitude of angels, angels upon angels, as far as the human eye can see the glorious figures of the tenants of the heavens, now made visible in His manifestation. They are a worshipping company.

We mention here the first chapter of Hebrews. "And again when he bringeth in the First begotten into the world (the inhabited earth), he saith, And let all the angels of God worship him." This is a quotation from Psalm xcvii. This does not mean the birth of Christ, for He was not then the First begotten, but the Only Begotten. He became the First begotten in resurrection. The bringing in of the First begotten is His second coming. Then the angels of God are worshipping Him and not only Him, but His body, His church as well. He is now glorified in His Saints. Each one is transformed into the same image. The blessed hope is realized, "We shall be like him for we shall see him as he is"; and He will be admired in all them that believed, in that day (2 Thess. i:10). In all the glories of that day, and in the events which are connected with it, angels are prominently associated. This is the teaching of both Testaments. Our Lord spoke of it on earth. The apostle Paul taught it. He speaks prophetically of the time "when the Lord Jesus shall be revealed from heaven with his mighty angels, in flaming fire, taking vengeance on them that know not God, and that obey not the Gospel of our Lord Jesus Christ" (2 Thess. i:7-8). An angel is seen standing in the sun inviting the birds of prey to the great judgment supper of God. They will be used by Him in gathering out the offending things from His kingdom, in separating the good from the bad. They will attend to the re-gathering of Israel. "He shall send his angels with a great sound of a trumpet, and they shall gather together his elect (Israel) from the four winds, from one end of heaven unto the other" (Matt. xxiv:31). No doubt in many other ways will the Lord use the angels.

When His kingdom is established upon earth, when the glory of the Lord will rest upon Jerusalem (Isaiah iv), when the glory of the Lord and the knowledge of it, not in a spiritual, but in a physical and visible way, will cover the earth as the waters cover the sea, there will be a wonderful intercourse between heaven and earth. No mind can imagine what it will be.

Up yonder in the sky, where we behold now the sun, the moon and the stars, telling out the glory of God, there will be seen the New Jerusalem. There is His glorious throne. From there, over the earth,* He reigns and His Saints reign with Him. The throne in the earthly Jerusalem is His likewise, for it is the throne of His father David. As Ezekiel tells us, a prince will occupy that throne and reign under Him (Ezekiel xliv:3).

Jacob, in his dream-vision, saw the angels of God ascending and descending on the ladder. The Lord Jesus Christ promised to Nathaniel and to His disciples

---

*It is not "on," but "over the earth;" this is the correct reading.

an opened heaven, "and the angels of God ascending and descending upon the Son of Man." It has never been in the past. But it will be in that day when He has been manifested. Heaven and earth will be joined together. The hallelujahs of the earth will be answered by the hallelujahs in the heavens and the message which the heavenly hosts uttered over the night-fields of Bethlehem is accomplished, "Glory to God in the Highest, Peace on earth and good will towards man."

* * * * *

Never before have God's people needed the vision of the unseen things and the believing anticipation of them so much as in our days. The playthings of the dust are being made more and more attractive by the god of this age to blind the eyes of them that believe not. We are, too, in constant danger to lose sight of the unseen things, because faith's vision becomes dimmed through the materialism of our times. For all we know, we are facing the first streaks of the coming day-dawn; the morning star is about to rise.

May it please our Lord to use these pages in refreshing our hearts as His waiting people, to fill us with holy anticipation, to guide our feet in the path of separation and to give us the courage of faith to go forward in His service, till the day dawns and the shadows flee away.

Things Hoped For

These are the crowns that we shall wear,
   When all thy saints are crowned;
These are the palms that we shall bear
   On yonder holy ground.

Far off as yet, reserved in heaven,
   Above that veiling sky,
They sparkle, like the stars of even,
   To hope's far-piercing eye.

These are the robes, unsoiled and white,
   Which then we shall put on,
When, foremost 'mong the sons of light,
   We sit on yonder throne.

That city with the jewelled crest,
   Like some new-lighted sun;
A blaze of burning amethyst—
   Ten thousand orbs in one;—

That is the city of the saints,
   Where we so soon shall stand,
When we shall strike these desert-tents,
   And quit this desert-sand.

These are the everlasting hills,
  With summits bathed in day:
The slopes down which the living rills,
  Soft-lapsing, take their way.

Fair vision! how thy distant gleam
  Brightens time's saddest hue;
Far fairer than the fairest dream,
  And yet so strangely true!

Fair vision! how thou liftest up
  The drooping brow and eye;
With the calm joy of thy sure hope
  Fixing our souls on high.

Thy light makes even the darkest page
  In memory's scroll grow fair;
Blanching the lines which tears and age
  Had only deepened there.

With thee in view, the rugged slope
  Becomes a level way,
Smoothed by the magic of thy hope,
  And gladdened by thy ray.

With thee in view, how poor appear
  The world's most winning smiles;
Vain is the tempter's subtlest snare,
  And vain hell's varied wiles.

Time's glory fades; its beauty now
  Has ceased to lure or blind;
Each gay enchantment here below
  Has lost its power to bind.

Then welcome toil, and care, and pain!
  And welcome sorrow, too!
All toil is rest, all grief is gain,
  With such a prize in view.

Come crown and throne, come robe and palm!
  Burst forth glad stream of peace!
Come, holy city of the Lamb!
  Rise, Sun of Righteousness!

When shall the clouds that veil thy rays
  Forever be withdrawn?
Why dost thou tarry, day of days?
  When shall thy gladness dawn?

—H. BONAR.